WEIRD CASES

Comic and bizarre cases from
courtrooms around the world

Gary Slapper

Wildy, Simmonds & Hill Publishing

First published in Great Britain 2010 by Wildy, Simmonds & Hill Publishing

Website: www.wildy.com

Slapper, G J

Weird Cases: Comic and bizarre cases from courtrooms around the world

ISBN 9780854900619

Printed and bound in Great Britain

PREFACE

Worldwide, the most bizarre aspects of human life fetch up in the law courts. Courts have seen judges do things such as try to turn off a musical tie playing "We wish you a merry Christmas" while sentencing a defendant to prison, fall fast asleep in the middle of trials, flip a coin to decide a case, demand a foot massage from a clerk, and get sentenced for judicial racketeering. Courts have seen advocates brought in to trials on stretchers wearing pyjamas in order to ask for a postponement, and try to pull an opposing counsel's arm out of its socket. Courts have seen a litigant sue for becoming pregnant by a stray sperm in a swimming pool, and a litigant suddenly strip naked before the judges. Courts have listened to the defences like that of a bogus dentist caught using DIY tools on his patients, a man who based his defence on being as hapless as Homer Simpson, and a woman who was running a brothel from an office in the criminal courts.

The courts have had to deal with situations such as a man called as a juror on his own trial for murder, a litigant fighting to call his child 4Real, and another trying to get the word lesbian restricted to mean 'resident of Lesbos'. The courts have had to pronounce on whether a lawyer is allowed to busk in the streets for money and how careful you need to be to avoid causing a partner injury during sex.

Courtroom drama is tense, compelling and mostly very serious. By virtue of having ended up in court, all civil and criminal disputes involve human beings in fraught situations. Mundane behaviour does not, by definition, get taken to court. The cases featured in this book are those that stand out as odd even among all the unusual dramas that challenge the courts.

This book arises from a weekly column called Weird Cases which I write for *Times Online*. I have been writing that column since 2007 and the cases here were first covered there. Here the stories are arranged in thematic chapters and I have aimed to give them some additional context.

ACKNOWLEDGEMENTS

I am deeply indebted to my family - Suzanne, Hannah, Emily, and Charlotte - for their enduring support. My interest in weird legal cases was developed when I noticed at dinner table discussions that these stories were greeted with considerably more enthusiasm than the thinly disguised lectures on commercial contracts or corporate law which I'd been running with limited domestic success for some years.

I owe particular thanks to Alex Spence, Law Editor of *Times Online*, who commissioned the column and has helped style it since 2007. I am much indebted for his punctilious editorial judgments, wry humour and encouragement.

I am very grateful to Abigail Bright, a future star of the Bar, for her excellent work in assisting with the arrangement of the cases. I am also grateful to Michael Herman who edited some of the columns, and to Frances Gibb and Clare Hogan at *The Times*.

I am much indebted to Andrew Riddoch, Commissioning Editor at Wildy, Simmonds & Hill, for his warm support, continuing interest, and encouragement. I am also very grateful for the vigilant copy editor professionalism of Heather Jones, and the graphic design work of Derek Brown. Thanks to Suzanne Harvey, photographed on the cover.

Many others have aided and abetted this venture in various ways. I thank my parents Doreen and Ivor Slapper, Clifford, Maxine, Pav, Anish, the late Raie Schwartz, David and Julie Whight, Carolyn Bracknell, Heather Montgomery, Hugh McLaughlan, Dr Anoop Nayar, Abigail Carr, Ben Fitzpatrick, Lynn Tayton QC, Frances Thomas, Carol Howells, Jane Goodey, Ken Shaw, Patrick Whight, Malcolm Park, and Dr David Kelly.

CONTENTS

Chapter 1

Every week a great many people slide into court either to do battle in a claim for compensation or court order or because the state thinks that they ought to be punished for a crime. The court is a theatre of calamity. With quiet deliberation, and controlled by thousands of legal rules, courts must often come to rational conclusions about events that would in fact be rejected by television drama producers as implausibly bizarre. In 1823, Lord Byron noted that "truth is always strange; Stranger than fiction". But in a good gloss in 1897, Mark Twain noted that the reason is "because Fiction is obliged to stick to possibilities; Truth isn't". No stage hosts more wayward truths than a courtroom.

Faking it

A key feature of any profession is that it restricts admission to those who have successfully achieved the required training.

Certainly, you'd expect that your dentist met that professional standard. But you'd be disappointed if you were a patient at the surgery of Alvaro Perez in Sampierdarena in northern Italy. Mr Perez, from Ecuador, was arrested in 2008 after his patients complained that he'd been knocking out their old fillings with screwdrivers and pulling teeth with household pliers. His main apparatus was a DIY power drill. Mr Perez was arrested after one patient suffered unendurable pain and summoned the police.

Perez, who has no dental qualifications, was charged with deception. There have been several comparable impostor offenders in Britain. In the world of medicine, there have been 40 cases in the last 70 years. In 1992, for example, Mohammed Saeed, a layman, was found to have been fraudulently practising as a family doctor in Bradford for 30 years. His partners had grown progressively suspicious of his absence of medical knowledge. He was given a 5-year jail sentence.

From the 1980s, Paul Bint, a former hairdresser, posed as a doctor in many hospitals for 12 years. He did all sorts of medical procedures – including trying to assist in a heart bypass operation.

In 1994, Roy Grimshaw, another fake doctor, was jailed for fraud after gaining a job as a clinical services manager at Guy's Hospital in London. He had previously posed as a surgeon at a private clinic in Lancashire, where he'd carried out nine surgical operations, many gynaecological procedures, and three vasectomies. He was only exposed when Bolton Magistrates' Court, where he was facing a driving ban, had his medical qualifications checked.

People have even been discovered faking it as lawyers. Say hello again to Paul Bint the former hairdresser and would-be doctor. He had also been convicted of fraud for posing as a barrister, having stolen a wig and gown and worked on his eloquence. His smooth speech though wasn't delivered in a courtroom but on a Virgin train in 2000. Proclaiming he was a distinguished advocate, he tricked the chief executive of Virgin, who happened to be travelling on the same train, into compensating him for expensive goods and tickets he claimed to have been stolen while on board.

Paolo Bonaccorsi was appointed as a senior governmental lawyer in Calabria, Italy, in 2001. It gradually became apparent, however, that he didn't know any law – and that proved to be something of an obstacle in the performance of his duties. Checks revealed that he was not registered as a lawyer and his legal qualifications were fakes.

But the prize for faking it so well that no legal proceedings followed exposure goes to Dr Kenneth D

Yates, an associate professor of physics at the University of New Hampshire in America. In 1954, 'Dr Yates' was revealed to be Marvin Hewitt, someone who had dropped out of high school with no qualifications but who had a teaching compulsion. When caught, he was in his fifth academic job in 7 years. He was not prosecuted because, despite his fraud, he was an admirable and respected physicist. Such dedication to physics isn't without precedent. It was Einstein who noted that he preferred equations to mundane matters of the present because "an equation is something for eternity".

Rough justice

In Escambia County Court in Florida, in 2009, Judge Patricia Kinsey ruled in the case of Albert Freed who sued a men's briefs manufacturer claiming he was injured on holiday by its badly designed underwear. He claimed the briefs "gaped open and acted like a sandbelt on my privates".

In a judgement she probably didn't anticipate making while at law school, Kinsey was required to engage in a detailed analysis of the relationship between male anatomy and male underwear. An alleged design defect supposedly exposed Freed to beach sand that had accumulated in swim trunks he was wearing over his briefs. Judge Kinsey doubted the contention that the briefs had opened "whereupon the edges of the opening abraded his penis like '"sandpaper belts'".

Why had Freed spent two weeks on holiday aggravating the problem without reporting it to his wife? He said he was so excited about this holiday to Hawaii – which he'd won – that he didn't want to complain about his debilitating pain until he had returned home. Asked in cross-examination why he hadn't inspected the problem early to assess the possible dangers, he replied that he was a "belly man" and could not see his penis.

The manufacturer called a scientist to show the briefs were safe but Freed, who represented himself, called no expert witnesses. The court, though, wanted some independent evidence about normal penile sensitivity and what was standard practice for men when adjusting themselves anatomically after donning briefs. Extraordinarily, the sole man among many female spectators in the public gallery was asked by the court for his opinion and he obliged. More extraordinarily, the law report notes that the man was "a prominent male criminal defence lawyer" who was just passing time in the gallery. The judgment thanks the lawyer for being a "good sport" in giving evidence and for his "surprisingly candid testimony" when answering intimate questions.

Judge Kinsey dismissed the claim, noting that Freed had failed to prove the link between his alleged injury and the briefs' design. "The uncontroverted expert testimony" she ruled "was that once a man's genitalia are adjusted in his briefs, 'vertical tension' is far greater than 'horizontal tension' and there is no tendency for the fly to 'gap'". She also said that Freed's peculiar method of dressing (he puts his briefs into his trousers and then pulls them both on together) might have aggravated his personal discomfort.

According to official data on accidents, underwear injures many Britons every year. In 2002, for example, 369 people were caused serious injury by underpants or knickers. Getting dressed or undressed in the dark or while impaired might explain those injuries. Less clear though is how 472 people were hospitalised by an item in the class "Hat, scarf, shawl, hankie".

To dye for justice

Do blondes *really* have more fun? Superior Court Judge Richard Gilardi had to consider the question in a case in 2008. There is no limit to the type of philosophical challenge that can confront judges.

In this American case, Charlotte Feeney was claiming damages from L'Oreal Inc. She claimed her natural blonde hair, the blondeness of which she had wanted to enhance, went dark brown after she used the defendant's hair product.

In her court depositions, Ms Feeney claimed she suffered sickness and acute anxiety when she saw her hair dark, and she then became clinically depressed. She contended she had suffered compensable loss because "blondes do get more attention than brunettes". She said her social intercourse had been impeded by her darkened hair.

The evidence that blondes have more fun is limited. Madonna once asserted that "the artifice of being blonde has some incredible sort of sexual connotation" but that wasn't based on a study that would satisfy a law court. In *Ministry of Defence v Jeremiah* (1979), Lord Denning acknowledged that "a woman's hair is her crowning glory ... she does not like it disturbed" – but he didn't let the law prefer blondes.

Ms Feeney's disaster came after she had purchased a tube of L'Oreal hair colour from a local supermarket in Stratford, Connecticut. Her friend helped her apply the colour but it soon became apparent that Charlotte's hair was turning brown. She argued that a brown colouring tube must have been negligently placed in a blonde product box. Her claim suggested that the hair colouring industry was obliged to put a warning on all boxed products explaining that the colour inside the tube might vary from the colour on the label.

L'Oreal contested her claim, arguing that a brown dye must have been purchased. It also entered the defence that, in any case, Ms Feeney wouldn't have suffered as she did if she'd have read and followed the packet's instruction to carry out a hair strand test before applying the colour to her hair. Ms Feeney said that it had become impossible to get her hair back to her natural colour. Her sworn statement informed the court "I stay at home more than ever in my life, I wear hats most of the time".

Shedding light where there was darkness, Judge Gilardi ruled that the claim must fail because it was completely unsubstantiated. He noted that "The plaintiff submitted no facts, no opinions and no standards" to support her claim.

This was not the first American case in which blondeness has been an issue. In a case from Hillsboro, Oregon, a witness giving testimony described the hair colour of someone he'd seen. To clarify what he meant, counsel asked him to point to someone in court with the same shade of hair. The witness said, pointing to a woman in court, "Well, something like hers except for more cheap bleached-blonde hair". The prosecutor then said: "May the record reflect, your honour, the witness has identified defence counsel as the cheap blonde".

Serial litigants

If you are appearing in court before magistrates in Hamburg and you have a legal argument against the way your previous cases were judged by the Bench, it is probably diplomatic to avoid arguing that the magistracy is "a bloody lazy bunch of layabouts".

Dieter Koehler, however, was not a diplomat and his abuse of the Bench in those terms was one of the errors that put him in jail for two weeks in 2009. In a series of over 200 court appearances in low-level cases that have wearied the courts for many years, Koehler has been indefatigable in his battles with various branches of civic government. In his last appearance before the Bench, he also repeatedly described magistrates as "the idiots". His accusation was that they were wasting the resources of the public purse by being incompetent – and not seeing things his way.

Dieter was a retired teacher who gave up teaching because he did not like children. Speaking after the case, a neighbour said that Dieter was often "very grumpy" and unlikely to be cowed by his custodial sentence.

The serial litigant is known in several jurisdictions. Omorotu Francis Ayovuare, a Nigerian-born surveyor, is probably Britain's most litigious man. By 2003, he had instigated 82 race discrimination claims, but won only two of them. In America, Billy Roy Tyler from Nebraska has described himself as the "greatest writ-writer in the world". He has sued a staggering range of people from his neighbour to the state governor. In the 1990s, he issued proceedings in 113 federal cases during one 2-year period. Both these prodigious plaintiffs, though, have been out-sued by Taso Hadjiev, 74, and his brother Asen, 75, from Malka Arda in Bulgaria. They began suing each other in 1968 in a dispute about a land inheritance from their parents. They are still at it, and have now litigated over 210 cases. They divided their family home with barbed-wire. A neighbour, Sabka Shehova, said: "They go to court for any old reason they can dream up – and none of it is ever true, they just want to sue each other".

A house divided

This isn't the first case of litigants who live under the same roof ensuring that while 'versus' divides them in court, a barricade divides them at home.

It isn't often, though, that a judge orders such a partition to be built but it has, on occasion, been done. In New York in 2006, Chana and Simon Taub were a couple going through a bitter divorce. For family and social reasons, they both wanted to remain in their house but were determined to divorce. The court heard their constant bickering and exchanges such as this one:

Simon:	She has 300 pairs of shoes.
Chana:	He has had my phone bugged. I'm not interested in shoes.
Simon:	Maybe it's 299, I didn't count.

Judge Sarah Krauss ordered the construction of a wall in the couple's house to separate them in their living areas.

Both for quarrelling brothers and former spouses, the subtleties of injunctions must sometimes give way to physical partitions. And anyway, the parties might agree with Cecil Graham in Wilde's *Lady Windermere's Fan*, who said, "I like talking to a brick wall, it's the only thing in the world that never contradicts me".

Sporting defence

When defence lawyer Carol Bickerstaff told Judge Paul Moyle in a case in April 2009, "Your honour, we now have the fashion police", she wasn't being metaphorical.

She was referring to the situation of her client, 17-year old Julius Hart, who had been arrested by police and put in the cells for the night for a fashion crime. He had contravened a local law in Riviera Beach, Florida, which has criminalised the wearing of trousers that sag significantly below the wearer's waist.

Police officers had arrested Hart for the "saggy pants" violation when they spotted him riding his bicycle while his low trousers revealed "4 to 5 inches of blue and black boxer shorts". Tired of seeing young people walking about town with their backsides hanging out, the older citizens of Riviera Beach had passed the clothes law in March 2009. For a first offence the fine is $150 or community service, the second time someone is caught with low trousers the fine is $300. In his defence, Hart observed that Prince Harry, David Beckham, and *High School Musical* star, Zac Efron, had all opted for a similar look. This established, Hart's lawyers claimed, that there was "nothing offensive" about the saggy look.

Hart escaped conviction by the skin of his low-slung pants. The judge ruled that the law prohibiting the trouser fashion was unconstitutional.

There are several places in America where similar local laws have been passed. In Delcambre, Louisiana, "sagging", as the revealing fashion is known, has been unlawful since 2008. It can attract a $500 fine and 6-moth jail sentence. Historically, the sagging style emanates from prison culture where inmates are not permitted belts.

Under an ordinance in Flint, Michigan, police have been issuing droopy-drawers tickets to local people since the early part of 2009. Police have even been supplied with a visual guide on enforcement: visible underwear warrants a warning, trousers falling below the bottom with underwear showing constitutes disorderly conduct. A substantially exposed unclothed butt will attract an indecent exposure charge (what legal theoreticians might refer to as the bottom line offence).

The English legal system has occasionally been confronted with incidents involving the revelation of a bottom but the courts haven't always been intolerant. In 1615, a court had to decide whether a Plymouth magistrate, James Bagg, could be dismissed for misconduct that included having protruded his bottom to the local mayor "in an inhuman and uncivil manner" and shouted "Come and kiss". He had been thrown out of office. The court held, though, that such conduct wasn't a sacking offence, and restored him to the magistracy.

In 1963, David Gaskell, the Manchester United goalkeeper, was prosecuted for making an insulting gesture to Sheffield United fans. Having saved a penalty, he swung round to the Sheffield fans, shouted a coarse two-word suggestion, then "turned his back on the crowd, bent forward, and slightly dropped his shorts exposing his bare buttocks". He explained to the court that he was merely "adjusting his shorts" which had sagged a little during his athletic dive to save the penalty. His defence in court was as good as his defence of the goalmouth – he was acquitted.

Wrestling with the law

A New Zealand telecoms firm, TeamTalk, was locked in a long legal dispute with radio communications company MCS Global Digital but, worried by the delays and costs of litigation, bosses from both companies resolved to use their own form of Alternative Dispute Resolution. In 2003, they agreed to settle the NZ$200,000 dispute with an arm-wrestling match. News, perhaps, as bad for lawyers as it was good for fitness centres.

The settlement of civil disputes through combat has a long history. It was approved in Europe from the 6th century by Gundobad, King of the Burgundians, and later endorsed by William the Conqueror for the use of Englishmen in disputes with the Normans. For infants, women, and persons over 60, professional pugilists or "champions" were often employed by the litigators to do their fighting for them. Some fighters got reputations like those of the finest QCs today. Thus, in 1220, 'Richard of Newnham' was the man sure to win your case for you, albeit with a weapon – a long stick. The church and some communities even had prototype in-house lawyers: permanently retained champions. The burden of proof was on the combatant who fought for an affirmative proposition, and his adversary won if the stars appeared before the fight was over.

In the New Zealand case, TeamTalk boss, David Ware, who made the challenge, lost his best-of-three bout against MCS chief Allan Cosford. He said losing was tough but "not nearly as painful as dealing with lawyers".

Law not written in stone

Steven Shaffer, described by *The Rural Democrat* as "a so-called historian", was, in July 2009, charged in America with the very rare felony of "removing an object of antiquity". He faced a possible 5-year sentence.

Although such a charge generally involves a small item like a goblet, this case concerns something significantly larger: an 8-ton boulder that Mr Shaffer is accused of removing from the bottom of a river running between Kentucky and Ohio.

The boulder is a huge piece of sandstone known as Indian Head Rock. It was given that name because it has engraved on it a face which some experts have said is an ancient petroglyph (a rock carving) by a Native American. The boulder was registered at the University of Kentucky as a protected archaeological object. It was once used as a navigation marker on the river. Historically, it became an attraction for local residents who would wade out into the river when the water was low in order to carve their initials on it. Most of the boulder, though, has been underwater since the 1920s.

In 2007, Shaffer worked with a diving crew to float the boulder and tug it to the shore on his side of the river in Ohio. His crew then raised it from the water using a crane and drove it to a municipal building. Shaffer and the Ohioans say the rock is more relevant to their history than that of their neighbour state's across the river. The Kentuckians disagreed and have prosecuted in what is, in effect, a vexed custody battle over a hunk of history. "There are other rocks in the river", Shaffer's lawyer, Michael Curtis observed.

Shaffer's prosecution would, his lawyer stated, involve proving that the 8- to 9-ton rock removed by Shaffer – which was stored in a garage in Portsmouth – was the one mentioned by historians as the Portsmouth Indian Head

Rock. When the judge was told at a preliminary hearing that the full trial would be likely to last for weeks rather than days he said to the defence lawyer "You've got to be kidding me?". The lawyer's reply was essentially: if you think the rock is voluminous wait until you see the documentary evidence we need to bring to court.

The case might look straightforward but some of the boulder's characteristics are not written in stone. One academic, for example, thinks that the face carving is not a prehistoric Native American work and is likely to have been executed with metal tools in the 19th century. An old philosophical conundrum asks what happens when an irresistible force meets an immovable object. That is an impossible question because it contains two contradictory ideas that cannot coexist. In court cases, though, there is no such thing as a permanent impasse – one side must eventually win. With luck in this case that will be before the boulder has turned into sand.

Please Sir, I want some more

When a County Sheriff sits in his office leaning back in a leather executive chair, the last place he would want to end up is incarcerated as a prisoner in one of his prison cells. That, though, is precisely what happened in 2009 to Sheriff Greg Bartlett from Morgan County in Alabama. He was sent to his own jail after a judge found that he had been starving his prisoners – in order to pocket money from their food budget.

Under an Alabama law passed in 1927, sheriffs were allocated $1.75 to feed each prison inmate per day. The sheriffs, though, were allowed to spend less than that full amount on prisoners' food and to pocket the difference. The sum of $1.75 bought a reasonable amount in 1927 but it doesn't over 80 years later. So, when Bartlett tried to maximise his profit turn from the $1.75, he took the idea of 'economic meals' further than the law permits.

Bartlett testified that, supplementing his annual salary of $64,000, he made an additional $212,000 in personal income over 3 years by siphoning off 'excess' from his prisoners' food budget. In 2001, in a federal legal action about conditions for Morgan County prisoners, a settlement was made which required inmates to be given the minimum of "nutritionally adequate meals". It was when a federal judge found evidence of continuing endemic malnourishment among prison inmates that he jailed the sheriff for contempt of court.

The judge heard how the sheriff had put about half of the public money allocated for prisoners' food into his own bank account while feeding 300 men and women prisoners things such as bloody chicken and cold grits. Ten emaciated prisoners testified before the federal judge saying things such as "we had an apple at Christmas and I think we had them one other time".

Bartlett has now been released and has moved back from his cell stool to his executive chair. There are, though, no reports on how well he dined during his prison stay. He has given the federal court an undertaking that in future he will spend all the public funding he gets for prisoners' food on prisoners' food. It remains to be seen whether the state of Alabama will now do anything about the anachronistic law under which sheriffs can pocket any public money that they don't spend on the designated purpose of feeding prisoners. A law that tempts officials to get rich by starving people is odd in the 21st century.

It is very rare for a person like Bartlett who works on the punishment side of the legal system to end up suffering under it. The most chilling case was that of John Stratford. He was a blacksmith who made a sleek new design of iron gallows for Norwich gaol in England. But then he murdered someone and, in 1829, became the first person to be hanged on his own handiwork.

Toilet language permitted in toilet

Does American law limit what a citizen can shout in her own home at her overflowing toilet? The answer, provided by Judge Terence V Gallagher, in a Pennsylvania case, is an emphatic 'no'.

In October 2007, Dawn Herb, from the city of Scranton, was cited for disorderly conduct when she was overheard swearing at her toilet as it overflowed through her home.

She had been heard by her neighbour, an off-duty police officer.

In *Commonwealth of Pennsylvania v Herb*, Judge Terrence V Gallagher found the defendant not guilty of violating a state law against obscenity. He ruled that that although her language may be considered by some to be "offensive, vulgar and imprudent", such representations are protected speech under the First Amendment to the Constitution.

Ms Herb settled a civil action against the city of Scranton, and the arresting officer, Gerald Tallo, for $19,000.

On the evening in question, when Ms Herb's neighbour heard her swearing near an open bathroom window, he shouted at her to be quiet. Oddly, for someone who proceeded to have Ms Herb prosecuted for profanities, her police officer neighbour had couched his instruction in the phrase "shut the fuck up". When Ms Herb advised him to mind his own business, he phoned a friend and colleague at the police department. Minutes later, two police cars were parked outside Herb's home, and she was facing up to 90 days in jail and a $300 fine. Herb, a mother of four, said, "At first, I just went inside and cried". She said, "I was thinking, 'How will I pay this fine?'". Her four-year old son developed anxieties that the police would take his mother away.

America has a good legal tradition of not allowing the law to close down the utterance of thoughts on the sole basis that they're rude or offensive. In *Cohen v California* (1971) the Supreme Court held that the state could not convict a person simply for wearing a swear word on his clothing. At the time of the Vietnam war, Paul Cohen had been arrested in a corridor of the Los Angeles Municipal Court for wearing a jacket bearing the words "Fuck the Draft". Justice Harlan ruled there was no case in such a situation for criminalising the "scurrilous epithet".

In 1722, James Sparling of Clerkenwell, London, was convicted of profanely swearing 54 oaths and 160 curses within 10 days. He was fined an absolute fortune (you can only imagine what he muttered under his breath when he heard the sentence). But his conviction was overturned because those writing the charge-sheet failed to record each of the alleged offending words.

Judges have not been averse sometimes to thrust and parry with those who use vulgar language in court. In one Canadian case, a judge in Manitoba gave a defendant a longer custodial sentence than he'd been expecting.

Judge: I sentence you to one year in prison.
Defendant: Well I'll be fucked.
Judge: Not for a year you won't.

All in the mind

In November 2008, Jerry Rose, from Nanaimo, Canada, sued those he holds responsible for an alleged theft of a computer technology he invented. His case is unusual.

First, meet the defendants. These included: Wal-mart, the Microsoft Corporation, Telus, the University of British Columbia, the British Columbia College of Physicians and Surgeons, and the Royal Canadian Mounted Police. Then, there is the sum of damages he is claimed: $2 billion. The nature of the alleged theft is also decidedly non-standard: Rose's claim asserted that he was subjected to "invasive brain computer interface technology, research experiments, field studies and surgery".

In a preliminary hearing, the judge was invited by five lawyers to dismiss Rose's 3-page claim as nothing more than a bizarre argument without any redeeming merit. The assertions about "brain-control", they said, were not supported by any plausible scientific evidence. The lawyer representing Microsoft said that Rose's action was akin to "someone saying they sustained injuries because their boat fell off the edge of the world". She said her client ought not to be subjected to a "nuisance lawsuit".

The judge, however, did allow the case to proceed. He accepted that Rose's case was "certainly an unusual one", but noted that in order to dismiss it he would have to be convinced there was *nothing* in the claim that could be litigated. The judge said he wasn't convinced of that. He referred to a precedent in which nine Canadians claimed they had been subject to mind-control experiments sponsored by the CIA at McGill University between 1957 and 1964. They were given LSD and put through some extraordinary brainwashing but didn't know they were part of an experiment. Their apparently bizarre allegation, though, turned out to be largely true. In 1988, the American Justice Department settled the case by paying the claimants $750,000.

Rose's case was eventually dismissed but he bounced back in 2009 with another claim this time against the Royal Canadian Mountain Police, the City of Nanaimo, the Attorney-General of British Columbia, Google, and his former next door neighbour. The saga continues.

None the less, most cases involving allegedly secret and mysterious operations eventually yield quite humdrum explanations once examined in court.

In 2000, magistrates in Sheffield, England, heard what happened after Gloria Havenhand was stopped by police for speeding. A man named Giles Norton marched into a police station in uniform, announced that he was Captain Crispin Cashmore from the Military Police and that Havenhand was immune from prosecution because she was working undercover on a clandestine surveillance mission for him.

A driver at the police station became suspicious because Capt Cashmore was not wearing the famous red cap of the Military Police, and he wasn't wearing a captain's three pips on his shoulder. When police officers checked with the captain's headquarters they found that there was no record of such a man. The magistrates found Norton guilty of obstructing police, and also of possessing two CS canisters, one of which was hidden in his sock. He was fined £600.

The true facts of the drama were more mundane. The lady charged with speeding wasn't Norton's special agent on a *Quantum of Solace* car chase. She turned out to be his mother. Norton had never been in the Military Police, either, although he did work in the general field of protection: condom machine sales.

The mother of all phone calls

Mothers have a particular keenness, of course, to speak with their sons regularly after they leave home. Cultures around the world recognise that. Hence the celebrated Jewish exchange when a son phones his mother after a long gap:

Son:	Mum, how are you?
Mother:	Very weak, I haven't eaten in 28 days
Son:	That's awful. Why haven't you eaten in 28 days?
Mother:	Because I didn't want my mouth to be full of food if you should call.

The law usually has no play in the mother–son relationship but when the maternal instinct went well beyond the normal in Austria in 2009, the matter ended in a court case. A mother who sustained a fusillade of daily phone calls to her son over a period of 2½ years was convicted of stalking him.

The mother was phoning her son dozens of times every day – 49 times on one of the days cited in the court evidence. The son, who initiated the proceedings, testified that he lived in a state of heightened anxiety as the phone rang throughout the day and in the night. The magistrates' court in the city of Klagenfurt fined her €360 and ordered her to desist from calling her son.

Star bucks

In the evident belief that Starbucks meant Easybucks, three men in California sued the corporation in 2008 after being asked an improper question on a job application form. They filed their case in a class-action seeking $26 million in compensation for 135,000 Starbucks job applicants.

The action was brought under the Californian Labour Code, which prohibits an employer from asking a job applicant about prior convictions for minor marijuana possession if those offences are more than 2 years old. Any job applicant who is subject to such an inquiry is entitled to compensation of $200. The three men sued and included in their action all those people who had applied for jobs on the same form since June 2004.

The application form did ask applicants whether they had *any* convictions in the previous 7 years but in a disclaimer on the other side of the paper, in very small type (8-point) and submerged in what the court found was "a veritable sea of boldface type", the form told applicants that the minor marijuana convictions needn't be disclosed.

The plaintiffs said that wasn't good enough. They argued the law had been broken because they had been unlawfully asked about marijuana convictions. They were entitled to $200, they contended, because the mere asking of the question was a violation of their rights. The part of the form saying they didn't need to answer was too obscure.

The men argued that by the time people filling out the application form got to the disclaimer saying they needn't fill in details of marijuana convictions, many of them wouldn't be bothered to go back and erase any conviction details they'd already recorded (even though it was only a 2-page form). Neither were they likely to ask for a new form. That, though, conjures up a picture of some extremely mellow and relaxed applicants.

The trial judge accepted the plaintiffs' arguments, and Starbucks appealed.

The appeal court dismissed the plaintiffs' case. It ruled the men did not have valid cases themselves so the whole class action fell. Of the three men, two had refused to answer the question and the third had truthfully said that he had no convictions. Their job applications were unsuccessful but not for reasons connected to drug use. The men also testified that, when they filled out their forms, they did understand they weren't legally obliged to reveal minor violations of marijuana possession.

The court ruled that a job applicant cannot recover damages, just because a form asks "an impermissible question", if he actually understands that he has no legal obligation to answer. The court said it didn't want to make a ruling that could create a whole new category of employment: professional job seekers whose quest is "to find (and fill out) job applications which they know to be defective solely for the purpose of pursuing litigation". It ruled that the law protecting people with old and minor marijuana convictions was not intended to be enforceable by "bounty hunters".

Mrs Cheveley, one of Oscar Wilde's inventions, in *An Ideal Husband*, says to Sir Robert Chiltern, "Questions are never indiscreet. Answers sometimes are". For Californian law, we need to modify that: some employers' questions *are* indiscreet, but they don't trigger cash prizes for unharmed litigants playing spot-the-mistake on application forms.

When the writ hits the fan

The law isn't only concerned with things of high intrinsic value. Occasionally, people sue over items the worth of which is high but not immediately obvious. In the case of Daniel Bennett, the item was 5st 7lbs of lizard excrement. Bennett sued the University of Leeds, in January 2009, for having disposed of the animal waste after he had meticulously collected it from remote areas in the Philippines as part of his doctoral research.

For 7 years, Bennett had engaged in a painstaking investigation into the diet, life, and behaviour of *Varanus olivaceus*, the very rare butaan lizard. His primary empirical evidence is in the form of the faeces that he collected from the jungle. After years of work for his doctoral thesis, Bennett had become an expert in his field. "I knew more about lizard faeces than I had ever thought possible", he declared. Giving background to the intensity of his loss, and the nature of the alleged negligence by his university, Bennett explained that he obtained his doctoral scholarship to pursue his study at Leeds "after 5 years of shit-searching".

Following an extended period engaged in fieldwork, Bennett returned to Leeds from abroad to find another student was occupying his desk space. He testified to the shock in seeing that while his personal effects had been carefully stowed in boxes "there was no sign of my 35kg bag of lizard shit". It might have been the largest collection of lizard faeces anywhere in the world, he noted, and said, "its loss left me reeling and altered the course of my life forever".

Bennett discovered that in the course of a space-saving measure, laboratory technicians had accidentally taken away all his biological evidence and incinerated it. He then waited 16 months for a formal response from Leeds. When it eventually arrived, it offered only £500 compensation and an assurance that new protocols would ensure the same sort of thing would not happen again. It was then that the writ hit the fan.

Bennett's bag of lost material carries particular significance because the hard-won evidence would be so immensely difficult to replace. The butaan is an extremely reclusive creature and the species is very difficult to locate. If these lizards ever encounter humans, they never return to that area.

The damages Bennett claimed were considerable and included money to reflect the loss sustained by the destruction of property used in the course of his professional work, and possibly any consequential shock. In 1938, the Court of Appeal recognised that compensation could, in principle, be awarded to someone who suffered shock from witnessing the loss of "something less important than human life". The court used the example of a "beloved dog". Whether that principle would extend to the biological matter lost in this case remains to be seen. It is new territory as people usually sue when the defendant's action has left them in the muck, not without it.

Credibility crunch

"Cap'n Crunch with Crunchberries" is a breakfast cereal. On the front of the packet, the beaming Cap'n is depicted thrusting a spoonful of colourful little balls of cereal at the shopper. But in 2009 Janine Sugawara organised a mutiny. In a putative class action, she sued the manufacturer for $5,000,000,000 for fraud, misrepresentation, and breach of warranty when she discovered the cereal balls were not fruity.

Sugawara had eaten the brightly coloured, sweetened corn and oat cereal for 4 years but argued that this was only because she had been deceived by the manufacturer into believing that the product contained fruit. Referring to the "crunchberry", the District Court for the Eastern District of California ruled that "there is no such fruit growing in the wild or occurring naturally in any part of the world", and so no reasonable consumer would be deceived into believing that the cereal contained "a fruit that does not exist". The court also noted that Sugawara didn't allege that anything on the packet was false – so there could be no finding of fraud. It held that for the claim to proceed, the court would have to "ignore all concepts of personal responsibility and common sense", and it wasn't going to let that happen.

Sugawara's failed action for fraudulent advertising compares with other curious cases in which the litigant took an advert too literally. Richard Overton from Michigan sued Anheuser-Busch, the manufacturers of Budweiser, for $10,000 for its beer adverts. One particular objection of his was the television advert for Bud Light involving two men, a beer truck and fantasies of "tropical settings, beautiful women and men engaged in endless and unrestricted merriment". He complained the advert promoted "impossible manifestations". In 1994, the Michigan Court of Appeals ruled that the fantasies represented in such adverts are not expected to stand up to the rational analysis of the courtroom. His claim was soberly rejected by the judges.

Unusual gene pool

A legal process in which paternity has to be identified generates some peculiar challenges. An entry under 'Father' on a recent Child Support Agency form allegedly says:

... I don't know the identity of the father of my daughter. He drives a BMW that now has a hole made by my stiletto in one of the door panels. Perhaps you can contact the BMW dealers in the area to see if he's had it replaced ...

Where the issue of paternity actually goes to law courts, the claims can be extraordinary. In the summer of 2009, a woman in Poland brought a civil negligence action in which she alleged that her daughter had been impregnated by a swimming pool.

Magdalena Kwiatkowska sought compensation having discovered that her 13-year-old daughter, whom she asserts has not had sex, became pregnant while on holiday. The mother says conception occurred after her daughter received a "stray sperm" in an Egyptian hotel swimming pool. Suing the hotel, the mother avowed that there is no way her daughter could have met any boys while on the family holiday.

Under Egyptian law, the owners of buildings owe a duty of care to people on their premises. And swimming pools feature in cases if they are alleged to be dangerously designed or maintained – but there is no case in Egyptian legal history of a swimming pool being accused of fathering a child.

The courts across the world have had to deal with some startling paternity cases, but one of the most extraordinary was decided in Missouri in 2007. A woman had sex, separately, with identical twin brothers on the same day, although neither man knew of the other's sexual encounter with the woman. She gave birth to a daughter but each brother claimed to be the baby's uncle, not her father. The woman identified Raymon Miller as the father but, objecting to making payment of $256 a week in child support, he argued his identical twin, Richard, was the father. Paternity tests using DNA samples revealed only that both brothers have over a 99.99 percent probability of being the father. The court accepted that even if the entire genome of the twins were sequenced, it wouldn't be able to identify the father.

Judge Copeland ruled that, in the light of the dual relationships, and based on the exact facts of each sexual encounter, Raymon would be held as the legal father of the child. Raymon made a stout counter-suggestion, saying of child support that "the state should eat it". The state, however, declined to take his advice and made a mandatory menu selection for Raymon who is now consuming humble pie.

Chapter 2

LOVE AND SEX

Mae West once observed that "to err is human – but it feels divine". Certainly, the strong romantic and carnal urges of men and women have lead to a remarkable and extraordinary variety of dramas being judged in law courts. What follow are some recent examples of such cases. The degree of general social knowledge about these things has advanced significantly since the Second World War. In a divorce case in 1948 the judge recounted various misunderstandings encountered among clients about the definition of adultery including "I did not think it was adultery during the daytime" and "it is not adultery if she is over 50".

Four weddings and an annulment

"I remember a nice blonde woman, and 28 days of partying and drinking". That much might have been heard before in court in Melbourne, Australia. But when it was uttered there in 2008 it wasn't during the manly pre-trial chat of two advocates reminiscing about their summer break.

This is the story of four weddings and an annulment. It was finally subject to judgment in June 2008 in the Family Court of Australia.

Mr Tristan – a pseudonym used in the law report – describes himself as "an old fashioned guy". He was married in 1966, but the marriage failed. He later met an Hawaiian woman, and fell in love. They got married and decided to live in Hawaii. But they were prevented from resettling by the US Department of Homeland Security, which revealed that the marriage to the Hawaiian woman was invalid because Mr Tristan was already married. When he pointed out that he'd been divorced from his 1966 wife, they said words to the effect: No not her, the second woman you married in Arizona in 1978.

It was at this point that a shocked Mr Tristan said he did dimly recall a "nice blonde woman" and a 28-day party in Arizona while he was on shore leave as an oil rig cook in 1978, but couldn't remember many details. Like Ross Geller in *Friends*, Homer Simpson, and Britney Spears, he seems to have been intoxicated by more than love when he got hitched in a walk-in marriage service. Shown the 1978 Arizona marriage licence by which he'd been wed to Ms Ernt (a legal pseudonym), he said "the sky fell in". He tried to track down his Arizona girl but could discover only that she had got married again in 1993, bigamously, as she had not previously divorced him.

At the Family Court, Justice Brown granted Mr Tristan an annulment of his 1978 marriage, saying that "he has no recollection of going through any ceremony of marriage ... or of discussing marriage, or of anything referable to marriage". That debauched revelry he'd attended in 1978 must have been quite a bender. Clearly, a party in Arizona is not something you'd want to attend if you had anything important planned for the next 28 days – or perhaps the rest of your life.

Historically, English law was quite strict in enforcing the law against bigamy, the offence of marrying someone while already married. In five cases for which there was a guilty verdict in 1753, for example, the punishment was branding. These days, the average sentence is 6 months.

But back in an age when, for the judiciary, political correctness meant opposing the vote for women, Lord Russell, the 19th-century Lord Chief Justice, was once asked what the punishment was for bigamy. Without any hesitation, the judge replied, "Two mothers-in-law".

Getting legal satisfaction

Recourse to law by disappointed people is extensive but some cases break new ground. In 2005 a Brazilian woman attempted litigation against her partner for failing to give her orgasms. The 31-year-old woman, from Jundiai, asserted in her case that her 38-year-old partner routinely ended sexual intercourse after he reached an orgasm. The claim was referred to a judge. As such a ruling required careful deliberation, there must have been hope in Brazil that the judge was not prone, in the phrase of Sir John Mortimer, QC, to premature adjudication. In English law there is no legal matrimonial obligation to provide the satisfaction that was being sought in Brazil. In the context of claims for marriage nullity, the courts have considered the orgasm but dismissed it as having no legal significance. In a 1952 judgment, elegantly garnished with Latin, the High Court held that the necessary and sufficient conditions of *vera copula* (true sexual union) were simply *erectio* and *intromissio*, which amount to nothing more than the act of intercourse.

Bare-faced cheek

"The priest concluded the ceremony and the couple were married", lawyer Alberto Figone told the court. Then, referring to his client, the bride, he continued, "but she was not able to take any proper photographs of the ceremony because she was semi-naked".

Semi-nakedness is an unusual feature of weddings at Chiavari on the Italian Riviera. So how the 30-year old bride came to be in this state was recounted in detail to Judge Pasqual Grasso at the civil court in Genoa. It was the key point of the case.

For most brides, the wedding day is of unparalleled importance. And the wedding dress is hallowed. The bride in this case was at the altar when the stitching on her expensive dress came apart and the dress slipped open, revealing her bottom to the whole congregation. The reactions among the 100 people in the congregation watching varied, but none of it was good for the unfortunate bride.

The incident occurred in 2006 but the matter only went before the court in the summer of 2008. The bride sued the dress shop in Rapallo for €23,000 compensation for financial loss and moral injury.

Wedding dresses have featured in various cases in different jurisdictions. In 2002, Jennifer Lucier Mora sued the Hyatt Tamaya Resort at Santa Ana Pueblo in New Mexico, alleging that it was negligent in failing to take proper steps to avoid disaster. A gust of wind had swept up her dress during the outdoor ceremony, and then her dress was run over by a golf cart which was a part of the wedding proceedings. Her claim was eventually settled out of court.

In 2001, Kirsty Adams spent months searching for the perfect wedding gown and eventually chose one for £2,000, which she ordered from a shop in Aberdeen. This was for her marriage to Douglas Reid at St Columba's Church in Elgin. The dress stayed intact for the ceremony but started to split immediately after the vows had been exchanged, so that her husband had to use various desperate manual techniques to prevent the dress disintegrating during the photo sessions. The shop owner defended the legal claim for compensation at Elgin Sheriff court, arguing that Mrs Reid must have treated the dress inappropriately. "You treat a wedding dress as a costume", the shop owner said, "not like jeans and a sweater". Sheriff Ian Cameron awarded the bride's mother, who paid for the dress, £500 damages saying that a wedding dress should do what is expected of it "which is different from a boiler suit but must last the course of one day's wedding activities".

Wearing a wedding dress, though, is no protection against the law. On 18 September 2006, in Sedgwick County, Kansas, Kandi Blakney went to the courthouse to get married. She arrived in her wedding dress. But when a court clerk entered Blakney's name in the computer for her marriage licence, two warrants for her arrest pinged up on the screen. The day did not end with her wearing a band of gold on her ring finger but two bands of silver on her wrists: she was hand-cuffed and hitched over to the county jail in her wedding dress on a $200,000 bond for probation violations.

To have and to keep under rap

People who declare they've had enough of their marriage and seek a divorce usually do it later in life than did an applicant to a court in 2009 in Jerusalem. She was 14.

The girl and her 17-year-old husband had married according to traditional Jewish law which requires three criteria to be satisfied. A wedding vow must be uttered in front of at least two witnesses, the husband must give his betrothed a ring, and the relationship must be consummated. The ardent couple satisfied all the requirements in a venture that began in a school playground. The ceremony was performed in front of a group of their friends but their parents, from devout religious families, were not present and only discovered the news later. Asking his daughter, "How was school today?" the father of the bride must have taken more than a moment to digest her unusual answer.

The wedding vow recited by the man at the ceremony, "Behold, you are consecrated to me by means of this ring, according to the law of Moses and Israel", does not need to be witnessed by a rabbi. The couple's union was later consummated – a liaison legal under Israeli secular law as sexual relations with a 14-year old are not criminal if the male partner is no more than 3 years older than the female.

The divorce proceeding was brought at the Rabbinical Court of Jerusalem, which granted the petition in April 2009. The Rabbinic Court Administration issued a statement saying that marriage was "a serious commitment that should not be taken lightly".

Meanwhile, 5,700 miles away in the Supreme Court of New York, a judge was presiding in another curious case about whether a couple had undertaken a serious relationship commitment with legal obligations. In this case, though, it was because the parties were *not* in a legally serious relationship at the material time that the claimant lost. Shaniqua Tomkins sued her former boyfriend Curtis Jackson, on the basis of an oral contract he'd allegedly made during an amorous conversation in a bedroom 10 years earlier. She claimed he had undertaken to take care of her for life if, as an entertainer, he ever "made it big".

The judge dismissed the case, saying that Tomkins' action was barred for being out of date, and, said that, in any event, "It is incredible that two then-unemployed, penniless, 21 year-olds would make such an oral contract". Jackson, though, did make it big. He is now the rapper known as 50 Cent but is worth over 800 million times his name.

Pimp my courtroom

What is the difference between a courthouse and brothel? Very little sometimes if allegations made in a criminal hearing in Ottawa are true. Laura Emerson, 28, stood accused by witnesses of using the courthouse where she worked as an employee, between October 2007 and July 2008, as the headquarters of her prostitute business.

Emerson was accused of luring and then forcing young women to become prostitutes, running the business from the court, and even taking calls from clients during the working day. That is something of a cue for cynical opponents of the legal system to observe that whether someone approaches the court as a defendant or as a customer, they'll end up being treated the same way.

According to one witness in the hearing, some of the young prostitutes were brought to the courthouse by Emerson so they could see her at work. Another witness testified under oath that she was recruited to work as a prostitute in an interview at the courthouse.

Emerson was prosecuted for several serious offences, including human trafficking. Her former boyfriend and co-defendant, Gordon Kingsbury, was charged with living on the avails of prostitution, sexual assault, and forcible confinement.

One witness testified that after she had been recruited to work at the sex business run from the courthouse, she would see up to ten clients a day in local apartments and be given crack cocaine by Emerson after every client "like my payoff".

The witness described occasions when she had tried to escape but had been caught and violently assaulted. Young women who worked for the business were allegedly subject to a savage regime. One of the girls abducted to work in the business had been held captive for a year.

Clearly, this is not an enterprise that deserves to have the courthouse as its administrative head office. From 1955, Canada did incorporate prostitution into legal, civil society when it decided prostitutes could be taxed and that there was no problem with the government taking that tax revenue and thereby benefiting from immoral earnings. But that was a court decision about a sort of prostitution that didn't involve human trafficking, kidnapping and violence.

Later, the Canadian courts even got precise about what a properly organised sex business in Vancouver could legally count as tax deductible expenses. A ruling decided that organisational payments made to bribe local police officers weren't tax deductible, but that money the business paid to lawyers to defend its girls was tax deductible. But running a sex business from the courthouse is taking things too far. Courts already have enough of a challenge defending slurs that they're venues for professionals living on immoral earnings without sex traders setting up shop under the same roof.

A family affair

Pleading guilty to a drink driving charge at Limerick District Court in Ireland in 2008, Fiona Porter, 24, put an unusual plea in mitigation. She explained through her lawyer, John Devane, that she had drunk alcohol on the evening in question in a distressed state after finding her husband in bed with her mother.

The court was told that after catching her husband Hugo, 34, and her mother Bernadette Garvey, 53, *in flagrante delicto* she learnt they'd been having an affair for 2 years. Mrs Porter went into a mental freefall.

The drink driving case was very serious as Mrs Porter was already banned at the time of the offence, but Judge Aeneas McCarthy acceded to her lawyer's request for leniency and spared her a custodial sentence. He suspended a 4-month prison term on Mrs Porter and banned her from driving for 6 years.

Then, however, the drama took another twist. "The way I feel about her this minute, I would stick a fucking knife in her", Bernadette Garvey said of her daughter. Ms Garvey denied the affair and declared, "I hate her and I wish to God she was dead for doing this to me".

After the court hearing, investigations revealed that on 28 June, the night Hugo Porter was alleged to have been in bed with his mother-in-law, he was in fact tucked up elsewhere, embraced in a most secure alibi: B-wing of Limerick Prison. He had been there since 31 May doing 6 months for a series of serious motoring offences.

But the case didn't end with that twist. Mrs Porter subsequently alleged that her lawyer is a liar. She said she'd actually caught her mother and husband in bed on 22 May, not on the June evening when she was stopped for drink driving, and that her lawyer knew that. Mr Devane denies he misrepresented his client and says he followed his instructions precisely. It remains to be seen whether the court will want this matter brought back for further consideration.

At the trial, neither Mrs Porter nor her husband gave testimony. Mrs Porter was exercising her right to silence, and Mr Porter was exercising in the local jail. It is difficult to know the truth at the heart of the dispute but I hope that the thoughts of a witness in an old English case don't apply. The distinguished Irish barrister Maurice Healy recounted that an English judge, Mr Justice Darling, once got very impatient with a witness from Ireland whom he suspected of not being fully frank. "Tell me" the judge snapped, "in your country, what happens to a witness who does not tell the truth?". "Ah me Lord" the witness replied with complete candour, "I think his side usually wins".

Wasting energy

Crime is a major problem in the United States. According to its national statistics, there are over 16,000 homicides a year, and over 800,000 aggravated assaults.

The authorities, however, do not spend all their time on such incidents, as Joanne Webb, a 43-year old married woman, discovered in 2004 when she was arrested and charged by two undercover officers in Cleburne, Texas. She faced a year in prison if convicted. Mrs Webb was accused of organising private parties to sell sex toys to friends. She was indicted for selling items "designed or marketed as useful primarily for the stimulation of the human genital organs". After some months of legal argument and public debate the prosecution was eventually discontinued.

The first conviction in a secular English obscenity case came in 1727 as immorality was seen to "disturb the civil order of society". Sending "obscene articles" through the post was legislated against in 1884. The Texan intolerance, though, is unmatched in modern British case law. Perhaps the state, concerned about economic productivity, is following the philosophy once espoused in an edition of the *Peking Workers Daily* in which sexual activity was denounced because it "consumes energy and wastes time" whereas, "love of the party and of the chairman, Mao-Tse-tung, takes no time at all and is in itself a powerful tonic".

An exercise in ambiguity

What is the difference between sex and Pilates? When a blind lawyer and a young actress fought each other in a 2009 lawsuit in Pennsylvania it was evident that not everyone can easily differentiate the two types of conduct.

John Peoples, a property and negligence lawyer who is legally blind, started using the services of Ginger Dayle in 2007. He paid with his credit card in her apartment by allowing her to enter her fees on credit card payment forms and then signing them under her guidance. He said that although he thought these were for sums of $275 an hour, the sum Dayle had actually written on the forms for 2-hour sessions was often $1,100. Altogether, he said, he'd been defrauded of $8,650 over 11 sessions. He sued his credit card company for failing to remove the disputed sums from his bill or to charge Dayle for them. He asked for over $1m in damages including compensation for emotional injury.

Dayle, who advertises herself as an actor, fitness instructor, professional dancer, and "adjunct professor", contended that the sessions with Peoples were Pilates lessons. Taken from the teaching of Joseph Pilates in Germany in the First World War, Pilates is defined by the *Oxford English Dictionary* as "a system of exercises designed to improve physical strength, flexibility, and posture". Peoples, though, was adamant that what he had received wasn't a series of muscular exercises. "I paid her" he testified "and she had sex with me". He stated that as he had arthritis and chronic fatigue syndrome the idea that he'd undertake systematic exercises for all his postural muscles was ridiculous.

Asked in a preliminary procedure whether, as a lawyer, he saw any problem with using the services of a prostitute, Peoples said that he was not worried because it did not affect the type of law he practised, and in any event prostitution was only a misdemeanour and would not trouble his professional disciplinary board. District Judge Edmund Ludwig dismissed Peoples' claim ruling that he could not recover the disputed charges because prostitution is illegal in Pennsylvania so the dealings were a "prohibited transaction" under the credit card company's contract with him.

Even where it is lawful, prostitution presents challenges to the legal system. In New Zealand in 2009, Logan Campbell, a taekwondo champion, was running a brothel in order to help fund his bid to participate in the 2012 Olympics. The New Zealand Olympic Committee (NZOC) sent him a "letter before action" threatening litigation unless he stopped linking the Olympic Games to his sex business. The NZOC said that prostitution is inconsistent with the Olympic values of "excellence, friendship, and respect". It's a moot point whether Campbell can be sued for doing something lawful. In any case, the ethics of the Games are usually derived from ancient Greece, and that was a society in which prostitution embraced *hetairai*, distinguished women held in high respect; higher perhaps than sports officials.

Injured in love

How good at sex is a person legally required to be? If, through lack of reasonable care, you injure your lover in a car accident or decorating incident, you are liable to pay compensation. What, though, if injury is sustained during carnal liaison? This question was answered in 2005 by the Massachusetts Appeals Court.

Early one morning, a man and woman in a long-term relationship were engaged in consensual sexual intercourse. During the passionate event, and, as the law report notes, "without the explicit prior consent" of the man, the woman suddenly manoeuvred herself in a way that caused her partner to suffer a penile fracture. Emergency surgery was required. Generally, under Massachusetts law, people owe others a duty of reasonable care to avoid injury. In this case, however, the court ruled that while "reckless" sexual conduct might be actionable, merely negligent conduct would not be. It dismissed the man's case. Justice Trainor noted that "in the absence of a consensus of community values or customs defining normal consensual sexual conduct" neither a jury nor judge could be expected to resolve a claim about whether any sexual activity had been executed with reasonable care. The 'Judicial Guidebook on Reasonable Sex' will therefore not be published anytime soon.

The 5-minute law

According to a regulation passed in 2002, women who wish to join the Indonesian military forces must undergo tests to ensure that they are virgins. Any legal disputes over the conduct or results of such tests raise issues that have been examined before by tribunals in other jurisdictions.

Under English law, for example, the minutiae of intercourse can be judicially examined to determine matrimonial status. A marriage which has not been consummated is voidable. Consummation occurs legally if there is sexual intercourse at least once. That sounds simple enough but the courts have developed a bizarrely detailed digest of rules to use when examining whether there has been such intercourse. An 1845 ecclesiastical court case asserts that the law requires penetration to a certain depth and for a certain duration. However, after an assiduous consideration of the details in a 1952 High Court civil case, the need for either party to have an orgasm was rejected. A man who engaged in coitus and "maintained that state of things for a period of four or five minutes" had done what the law required.

Not fair game

It was announced in May 2000 that Jim Hodkinson, chief executive of a major fashion company, had been sacked for "groping" a female employee. He was said to have "touched up" one of his employees at an awards dinner. This was the first time that anyone in such a senior position was publicly dismissed for inappropriate sexual behaviour. The way employment law treats cases of sexual harassment has changed admirably in recent times. Thus male employers are no longer permitted to regard female employees as fair game.

For some employers the *ius prima noctis* (right of the first night) or *droit de seigneur* (right of the lord) might have gone but the social legacy remains. These medieval rights allowed the lord to share the bed of the bride of any one of his vassals on the wedding night. Sometimes the vassal only got to enter the wedding bed after the lord was leaving it but more often the right was used as an excuse for levying dues. Lawyers themselves cannot claim, though, to have always behaved in an impeccably chivalrous way. When the Old Hall at Lincoln's Inn was re-built in 1490 it was partly paid for, according to an excellent history by Sir Robert Megarry, by fining barristers 6s 8d for "fornicating with a woman in chambers". Intriguingly, the fine rose to 20s "if he shall have or enjoy her in the garden or Chancery Lane".

The price of love

Andy Hoyle, 35, from Wrexham was inundated with offers in 2003 after putting his wife up for auction on the internet. He advertised Mel, 30, on eBay with the words "The chassis is in excellent order for the mileage, and warranty given at extra cost".

In the centuries before legal divorce was available to most people, however, the auctioning of wives was a popular way to dissolve broken marriages. Such 'wife-sales' were run in market squares from the middle ages until 1887. The sales were not legal (Lord Mansfield regarded them as criminal conspiracies) but were generally tolerated by the authorities. On 18 July 1797, *The Times* reported the case of a butcher who "exposed his wife to sale in Smithfield Market, near the Ram Inn, with a halter about her neck, and one about her waist which tied her to a railing". In that case "a hog driver was the happy purchaser, who gave the husband three guineas and a crown for his departed rib". Such sales, however, depended on the wife's consent, and the purchasers, who were arranged in advance, were normally the women's paramours.

To be taken twice a day

In 2009, the US Tax Court ruled that money spent on prostitutes and pornography is a not tax deductible expense, even for a New York attorney.

William G Halby, an established Brooklyn tax lawyer, had submitted to the Internal Revenue Services a range of expenses he wanted deducted from his tax liability as "medical expenses". Under section 213 of the Internal Revenue Code, expenses for medical care can be deducted from a tax liability if the care was for the "diagnosis, cure, mitigation, treatment, or prevention of disease" or for the purpose of "affecting any structure or function of the body".

Halby argued in this case and a previous one that his sex expenditure was made both to treat disease and to improve some aspects of his anatomical functionality. He didn't skimp when buying his medicine – in 2002, for example, he sought to deduct $111,364 from his tax liability for money spent on "therapeutic sex" in order to "relieve osteoarthritis and enhance erectile function through frequent orgasm". In 2005, his claim for tax deductions included $5,005 for sex books, magazines and videos, and $42,152 for prostitutes. For tax purposes, Halby kept a record in his personal journal of all visits to his "service providers" and of all the literature and equipment he bought including a claim for condoms and (unprecedented in American tax law cases) a claim for "nipple clamps".

When almost all of his claims for tax deductions were refused, Halby brought a case against the Commissioner for Internal Revenue in the tax court. Judge Goeke noted that none of the alleged sex therapy had been prescribed by a doctor. In any event, the court ruled, in New York patronising a prostitute is illegal (section 230.04 of the New York Penal Law) and you cannot claim tax deductions for illegal medical treatments. Similarly, the pornography was for Halby's "general welfare" not on prescription for any specific ailment.

While lawyers cannot claim expenses when they hire prostitutes, prostitutes can claim expenses when they hire lawyers. In 1964, the Court of Exchequer in Canada had to decide which of the expenses of running a call girl business in Vancouver were tax deductible. A claim for $1,925 for the business paying its lawyers was allowed by the court – happily, law courts are good places in which to plead the universal necessity of lawyers. However, the court did gently reject a separate claim of the call girl business to reduce its tax liability by another $16,500 – the money it had paid to police as "protection fees".

The tables of love

Adopting a policy that "family law must be updated to ensure that it reflects the needs of all our people", legislation from the Scottish Parliament has accommodated all possibilities. It includes sections that permit a man in Scotland to marry his mother-in-law or daughter-in-law, and a woman to marry her father-in-law or son-in-law, if death or divorce has ended the original relationship. Marriages between people sharing blood, like siblings, have been banned for "consanguinity" since ancient times although the scope of the genetic principles has not been precisely formulated. Additionally, marriages have been banned for "affinity" between close non-blood relatives – like the 'man to mother-in-law' example – and this is the principle now being altered in Scotland. Based on biblical lines, like that in Leviticus 20:14 which says if a "man takes his wife and her mother", all three shall be burned alive, the prohibited degrees of affinity were introduced into law in Britain in legislation from the Marriage Act 1540. There was no particular science behind the old lists of prohibited degrees of affinity. According to one classic history, they were simply the "idle ingenuities" of men who liked drawing up tables and "doggerel hexameters".

The bonds of marriage

The law favours attempts at matrimonial reconciliation but not in all circumstances. In 2009, after 7 years of marriage, Helen Sun was getting tired of her husband not listening to her. In an effort to get his undivided attention, however, she embarked on a legally unconventional scheme. While he was asleep in bed she handcuffed him to her and hid the key.

When her husband, Robert Drawbaugh, awoke he didn't take well to her new form of conversation encouragement. When he said that the arrangement wasn't his idea of being locked in an interesting discussion, the exchange with Sun swung into the sort of violent spectacle Romans watched in the coliseum.

The criminal justice system in Connecticut, where the couple lived together, became involved when the handcuffed Drawbaugh managed to pin down Sun long enough to use his mobile to call 911. The dispatcher taking his details heard him repeatedly scream in agony as his wife frenziedly bit and gouged him with her teeth in a struggle to stop his call. Asked by the dispatcher why his wife was attacking him he replied that it was because he was divorcing her. The dispatcher kept the call going while the police sped to the house. Screeches of pain were audible throughout the 5-minute 911 call as the biting continued, and Drawbaugh pleads, "Are they almost here? Oh God. I need help!".

The police eventually arrived, broke in through the front door and rescued Drawbaugh. Sun was charged with assault, disorderly conduct, reckless endangerment and unlawful restraint and stood trial at Bridgeport Superior Court.

The civil court in Bridgeport, where a divorce petition had been filed, was the venue of proceedings for dissolution of the marriage. It seems unlikely that any reconciliatory programme will have been suggested by the Bench.

The courts have dealt with some curious claims arising from attempts at reconciliation by estranged spouses. In some jurisdictions, there was a rule that, if a husband had sex with his wife after he became aware she had slept with someone else, he was taken to have condoned her errant conduct and absolved her. In trying to get around that rule for a divorce-seeking husband in New South Wales in 1888, a lawyer called Moriaty argued to the court a theory of "without prejudice" intercourse. The theory was that the man was entitled to have sex with his once-wayward wife on a sort of experimental basis to see if he could recover his feeling for her. That sex, argued the lawyer, shouldn't be taken a proving a reconciliation; it should be without prejudice to whatever the husband would finally decide.

Whether Moriaty had drafted a letter headed "without prejudice" for the husband to hand to his wife just as they embarked upon a carnal rapprochement is not stated in the law report. In any event, the court wasn't keen on the theory, denouncing it as a "disgusting absurdity" and "an outrage upon morals".

When law is hard to swallow

Ingrid Bergman once described a kiss as being "a trick designed by nature to stop speech when words become superfluous". It was such a kiss that featured in a major legal dispute in 2009 but far from having made words superfluous, the kiss in question generated thousands of them as they flew from lawyers' keyboards in France.

The dispute began when the international tennis star Richard Gasquet tested positive for cocaine and said that he must have absorbed the drug during passionate French kissing with a woman he had met the previous evening.

During an international tournament in Miami in March, a woman known only as Pamela in later legal papers, was in a restaurant when in walked the glamorous French tennis player. They struck up a friendship which quickly turned romantic as they went on to a bar and then a strip club. According to Gasquet, they exchanged many French kisses, "and good ones, too" in his phrase. The following day in a random test, Benzoylecgonine, a metabolite of cocaine, was detected in Gasquet. After hearing much evidence about the romantic encounter, a tribunal of the International Tennis Federation (ITF) found that Gasquet and Pamela kissed "at least seven times, each kiss lasting about five to ten seconds".

The tribunal found that, on the balance of probabilities, the cocaine detected in Gasquet's urine sample had entered his system "by means of Pamela's kissing". The judgment declared that it was not unnatural for Gasquet to have been attracted to kiss Pamela, and it imposed the minimum sentence of a 10-week ban. The ITF will appeal against that sentence at the Court of Arbitration for Sport, arguing 10 weeks is too lenient (the maximum suspension is 2 years).

French police had undertaken a scientific test of hair from both Gasquet and Pamela and the results, leaked to the press, showed that she was a regular cocaine user and that he was not. Two cases were triggered: he filed a private prosecution against her for the administration of a harmful substance; and she sued him for defamation for his depiction of her as a sexually promiscuous drug-addict. She admits past drug use but says she is now reformed. In any event, the litigation ensured that the world's 38th best male tennis player was about to spend less time playing on courts and more time arguing in them.

The defence of involuntary drug ingestion through close contact with another has been argued before. In a case from Monterey, California, a man who had tested positive for cocaine was challenged by counsel to explain the presence of the drug in his urine sample. He said that he had picked up a woman in a bar and had gone back to a hotel room with her where she had administered the drug to herself intimately and had later invited him to perform oral sex. It was during that act of passion, he contended, that he must have unintentionally absorbed the drug.

Aural sex

How noisy can sex get before it is illegally loud? A jury in a case in Newcastle Crown Court has had to decide this challenging question.

In April 2007, neighbours made many complaints against Caroline Cartwright about her ecstatic screaming during sex with her husband. Council environmental officers were dispatched to set up recording equipment in a neighbouring property to measure the level of shrieking, moaning and, evidently, slapping that could be heard through the walls and outside on the street. The recorded noise levels were unacceptably high, so the council imposed a noise abatement order on Cartwright.

But the loud sex continued, unabated, so Cartwright was prosecuted. In 2009, at Houghton le Spring Magistrates' Court in Sunderland, she was convicted of breaching the abatement order. Giving testimony in court, a neighbour stated that not only was the sound of the sex excessively loud, penetrating a wall that she had had soundproofed, but it was maintained with some stamina. The witness said, "when I first moved in it would start around midnight and last until 3am–4am".

The lawyer for Cartwright said, "she believes the way she performs is natural and normal". The court disagreed. The chair of the Bench told the defendant, "you could have minimised your vocalisation while having sex". It convicted Cartwright and sentenced her to a £200 fine and a 4-year Anti Social Behaviour Order (ASBO) banning her from "making excessive noise" anywhere in England.

But she still failed to quieten down. She said "Effectively, they are trying to ban me from having sex". Cartwright asserted that she could not control the noises she made during sex and noted, "we are just expressing how we feel. If they want to lock me up for it they can".

The very next day, she was arrested again for making too much noise, and then further arrests followed twice in the following week. Each arrest arose from highly audible and resonant early morning moaning and groaning and the sound of a bed banging against a wall. After the third arrest, she was charged with breaching her ASBO and stood trial before a judge and jury in Newcastle. She was refused bail and was remanded in custody.

The courts have rarely been asked to rule in a case where the sound of female sexual rapture is a legal issue – but it has happened. In October 2007, at the magistrates' court in Ipswich, Queensland, the humdrum proceedings were interrupted at one point by the sound of a gasping female voice in an advanced state of excitement. The sound from the court gallery was exclaiming, "Oh yeah ... yeah ... oh yeah ... do it to me". An over-optimistic male advocate in mid-argument might have smiled bashfully at the Bench and wondered at the power of his eloquence.

But whatever the woman was enjoying it wasn't a legal speech. Her voice was just the hi-fi ringtone on the phone of a man in the public gallery. As the sounds of ecstasy became progressively louder the court proceedings froze. The man with the extraordinary ringtone fumbled desperately to turn off his phone. He was identified and told he could be held in contempt of court and imprisoned, but the magistrate ultimately exercised mercy. One missed call, one missed cell.

Sexual healing

In Kenya, James Kimondo broke new legal ground in 2009 by suing the leaders of a coalition of women's groups for the absence of sex in his life.

In a bid to pressure Kenyan political leaders to put their differences aside and act for the common good, a consortium of women's groups known as "G10" organised a boycott of sexual relations with men. Their argument was that men should not have time for carnal relations while their country was disintegrating through economic and political problems. The background to this campaign was that in 2008 the country's president and the main opposition leader had been guided by mediators into a power-sharing government but the politicians' continuing mutual hostility fractured the coalition. Widespread disorder followed.

The sexual abstinence pledged by the women's groups clearly had some effect on Mr Kimondo's life. He issued civil proceedings for damages in the High Court in Nairobi, asserting that his wife had refused to honour his conjugal rights because of the campaign. He sought damages for "anxiety and sleepless nights".

"I have", he claimed, "been suffering mental anguish, stress, back aches, [and] lack of concentration". His writ contended that he was a happily-married man until 29 April 2009 when the women's groups called for a 7-day abstention from sex. Kimondo did not get injunctive relief from the judicial chamber; what remedy, if any, he obtained domestically is not recorded.

Whether an absence of sex for 7 days is a legally actionable wrong is not specified in most countries. In England, the matrimonial obligation is simply to maintain a "mutually tolerable sexual relationship", although even that does not apply across the life of the marriage. The ancient maxim of "twice a week", expressed in the delicate Latin and Greek maxim *bis ruere in hebdomade* (to disturb twice in seven) is not law. As Lord Merriman said in a case in 1947 – and he'd heard more than a few colourful witness testimonies in his decades as an advocate and a judge – "there is the greatest diversity of standards between one set of spouses and another as to what is a normal standard of sexual intercourse".

In 1960, the Court of Appeal ruled that a wife from Croydon was in breach of her marital obligations when, with great intolerance towards her husband who wasn't as sexually charged as she was, she repeatedly badgered him for sex. To rouse him into copulation she would, in the early hours of the morning, "pull his hair, catch hold of him by the ears, and shake his head violently to and fro". By eventually conceding to her demands, though, he was judged to have condoned her cruelty.

Good love, bad love

The Californian Court of Appeal ruled, in January 2009, that a Lutheran school acted lawfully when it expelled two girls for "conducting themselves in a manner consistent with being lesbians".

The girls, under the legal names Jane Doe and Mary Roe, had sued the school in Wildomar for discrimination, invasion of privacy, and unlawful detention (being held in a room for hours while interrogated about their sexual orientation). A fellow pupil had told a teacher that one of the girls had said she loved the other. There then followed an inquisition by teachers to discover every fine detail of how that love manifested itself. Was it, in the eyes of the school, a good sort of love or a bad sort of love?

The school's investigation included inspecting the MySpace pages of the girls. Teachers tried to decide what they might infer from the fact that one girls said of her sexual orientation "not sure" and the other one's site indicated she was "bi" (although that was said to have been added by a friend). The court report notes that the girls' MySpace names were "Scandalous Love!" and "Truely [sic] in ♥ with you". In the proceedings, the school tried to get from the girls their sworn answers to a series of carefully drafted questions from lawyers such as "Who did you go to the prom with?".

In the end, although no evidence of any physical relationship was discovered, the school took the view, in somewhat medieval language, that there had been "a bond of intimacy" between the girls and that this was "characteristic of a lesbian relationship".

The headteacher claimed that the girls had told him they had hugged and kissed each other, although the girls denied they had ever said that and asserted they'd only reported their love for one another.

The trial court took the view that the discrimination made by the school was lawful because, although

Californian law prohibits discrimination in a business context, the school is not a business. The appeal court supported that analysis. It ruled that the expulsions were justified because the school treats homosexuality as a sin and prohibits all "scandalous conduct" on or off the school premises.

Perceptions have shifted a lot in the last 50 years. Today, in the Jane and Mary case, the authorities were fervent in investigating all aspects of the girls' relationship, and they let their suspicions trump the denials of the girls. By contrast, in a case in 1954, a judge refused to grant a divorce where a wife had a relationship with another woman whom she often "kissed on the lips", and with whom she often spent the night in the same bed "in the wife's bedroom in the vicarage". The befuddled judge simply said this was all "a very odd business" but was "perfectly innocent".

Keeping a judge's chamber out of the news

In 2008, the Romanian Constitutional Court quashed an attempt by the legislature to make the news media broadcast equal measures of good and bad news.

Politicians in Romania said that too much bad news was being reported and it was bringing people down. Bemoaning the negative effects of bad news on "the health and life of the people", they successfully put a law through the Romanian senate stipulating a principle that required radio and television companies to broadcast one good news story for every bad news story.

The law was sponsored by senators from the National Liberal Party and the far-right Great Romania Party and passed by the Romanian senate. What was needed, the politicians enthusiastically agreed, was less news about depressing things (like incompetent or sinister politicians) and more news about cheery things.

They legislated that the National Audiovisual Council would need to judge what was positive news and what was negative news. The chairman of the council, though, was understandably perplexed. He pointed out that such a half-good and half-bad recipe for all news broadcasts would be impossible. He said "News is news. It is neither positive nor negative. It simply reflects reality".

The opposition liberal democrats argued that the 'good news' law was unacceptable as it restricted freedom of expression. The court agreed, and declared the legislation unconstitutional. That, of course, is good news for democracy.

English law has been disinclined to control the news, despite even judges having been sometimes troubled by journalists. In *Mason v Mason*, a case about a couple from Basingstoke, the Court of Appeal ruled that it wasn't "unreasonable behaviour", for a wife to ration her husband to sex once a week. The Lord Chancellor, Lord Hailsham, said after the case that he didn't mind the cheeky newspaper headlines which said things such as "Sex once a week enough, appeal judge says" (*The Times*, 5 December 1980), but he did object to the newspapers that tried to get interviews with the wife of the judge.

Chapter 3

FOOD, DRINK AND DRUGS

A s food is such a regular and indispensable part of the behaviour of people it isn't surprising that it features in unusual ways in legal cases. But, of course, it is not all that people ingest. As the American writer Fran Lebowitz noted, "food is an important part of a balance diet". Alcohol is enjoyed by many people, although not necessarily as much as it was for WC Fields who said "I always keep a stimulant handy in case I see a snake – which I also keep handy". Drugs, similarly, seem to be in widespread use in many parts of the world; PJ O'Rourke observed that "drugs have taught an entire generation of American kids the metric system".

Taking the fizz

While all agree that the resources of the criminal justice system shouldn't be abused, not everyone shares an understanding of what counts as enough of an emergency to summon the police. In Boyton Beach, Florida, Jean Fortune was summoned to court in February 2009, after he called 911 because his local Burger King had run out of lemonade.

Fortune arrived at the drive-thru restaurant hungry after work and placed his order. He got into an altercation with the cashier when it turned out that the restaurant had no lemonade. He dialled 911, then, while the police were on their way, he kept the emergency service operator on the phone in a detailed conversation about his fury with the customer service at the burger bar. When then nature of the crisis became apparent to the operator she gave him explicit advice: "customer service is not a reason to call 911. 911 is for if you're dying. OK?". But Fortune persisted in his angry outrage.

The affidavit filed for the court by the police officer who attended the lemonade crisis notes that Fortune was "unhappy with his order" and had complained that it was taking too long to cook. Then, the affidavit notes, Fortune "became irate when there was no lemonade". He was charged with misuse of the 911 communication system, which, upon conviction, can attract a custodial sentence. Whether the court's canteen reviewed its soft drinks stock in preparation for Fortune's appearance isn't certain.

Meanwhile, 5,200 miles away, in Warsaw, Poland, police were preparing similar charges of wasting police time against Lukasz Zapalowski for an emergency call he had made. Zapalowski, a 22-year-old student, had phoned the emergency services to report that he was being subjected to "psychological torture". Police rushed to rescue him but it turned out that the alleged torturer was his mother. Zapalowski said he'd been impelled to make the emergency call after his mother's regular and unrelenting demands that he should take a bath once a week and tidy his room.

In Britain, cases of misuse of the emergency services system have included a woman who phoned to demand help for the hamster that was trapped behind her wardrobe, a man reporting that his wife had got on the wrong bus after a shopping trip, and a woman desperate because she couldn't find a DIY store. The lost woman is recorded as saying, "Help me – I've been driving around Huntington for an hour now and I can't find Homebase". When the operator explains that such a situation is not, legally, an emergency, she replied "I know that, but honestly, I'm nearly in tears". Last year, in New Zealand, Arthur Cradock was prosecuted for wasting police time following an emergency call in which he exclaimed that he was being raped by a wombat. Cradock was sentenced to 75 hours' community service after he testified that the marsupial's sexual predation had left him with no anatomical injuries although, he asserted, it had traumatised him into speaking with an Australian accent.

This one's on me

When James Doherty, 57, stood before Justice Deborah Austin in court in Ontario, Canada in 2008, and said, "I know it sounds bizarre but ...", he was following an extensive line of defendants worldwide who have proffered unusual excuses.

His story, though, by most standards, was rather odd. He had been stopped by police officers after a report of "an impaired driver" in the district of Forest, where two "stag and doe" celebrations had been taking place. Mr Doherty conceded that his blood-alcohol level was twice the legal limit when he was arrested. But he said the real reason that his judgment might have been impaired was that he had been struck by lightning. It wasn't so much that he'd hit the bottle as that he'd been hit by the weapon of Zeus.

Justice Austin said it was one the most unusual explanations for poor judgment she had ever heard. Doherty acknowledged previous convictions for impaired driving during the 1980s and early 1990s (although he didn't furnish the court with meteorological records to explain earlier events), and he was jailed for 30 days. How far the rapid consumption of strong liquor can leave someone feeling electrocuted was not a matter investigated by the court.

There have, though, been drink-drive defences just as unconventional as that of Mr Doherty. For example, arrested for driving while being four times over the blood-alcohol limit in 2002, Douglas Harvey, of Glenrothes, explained that although he had not imbibed too much whisky, an unusual condition from which he suffered meant that his liver actually produced alcohol. Although the science to support the "human-distillery" theory wasn't furnished on Perth Sheriff Court, Mr Harvey volunteered to undergo surgery to prove his claim. But, after letting the offer rest on a knife edge for a while, he changed his stance before any explorative surgery was commissioned by the Bench, and pleaded guilty to two drink-driving charges. He was banned from driving and fined £450.

In Australia, in 2007, when caught driving five times over the limit, Stephen James Diggs, told Darwin police officers simply "We were hunting pigs ... I had a few beers, bro". But he later elaborated and raised an unprecedented mosquito defence. He said that, while on the hunt, he had run out of insect repellent spray, and his drunken journey by car became necessary to avoid a swarm of savage mosquitoes. He escaped the bites but not a conviction.

The real thing

In 1920, Coca-Cola sought an injunction to prevent a rival company from selling a drink called Koke. The injunction was upheld by the US Supreme Court. The Koke company argued that the Coca-Cola should not be protected by the law because it was falsely representing that its drink contained cocaine. Justice Holmes acknowledged that, in earlier years, the drug had been used in the drink. He said in his ruling that "Before 1900 the beginning of the goodwill was more or less helped by the presence of cocaine, a drug that, like alcohol or caffeine or opium, may be described as a deadly poison or as a valuable item of the pharmacopoeia according to the rhetorical purposes in view". By much earlier than 1920, though, cocaine had been eliminated from the drink, and a picture of coca leaves and cola nuts on the label did not, it was decided, mislead most people.

Fired without smoke

Legislation making it unlawful to smoke in public places now exists in many countries – such as Ireland, the UK, and France.

In some parts of America, things have been taken a bit further. In California, from 2008, it has been an offence to smoke in a car in which a minor is present, and, in many states, employers are screening job applicants to see if they are smokers.

The American company Cleveland Clinic, for example, does health tests on job applicants, including a screening for nicotine. If you test positive, you're not shortlisted for interview. The company Scotts Miracle-Gro, an Ohio-based lawn company, conducts random urine tests on its employees to ensure none have started smoking. Companies whose employment conditions include a ban on workers smoking at home or away from work have fired people who break that condition.

In 2008, though, an employer in Germany approached things from another point of view. Thomas Jensen, head of a telesales company in Buesum, was being taken to a tribunal for firing *non-smokers* and replacing them with smokers who "fitted in better".

The company laid off three non-smokers and said it would not be hiring any more people who don't smoke. Mr Jensen said, "Smokers have always been our best employees. Non-smokers interfere with corporate peace".

German law forbids smoking in pubs and restaurants, but permits it for people working in small offices. Mr Jensen said of the dismissed non-smoking staff, "They just complained all the time about smoking, and I don't like grumblers".

Across the world, people have been told they aren't wanted by employers for all sorts of reasons: because they're too old, too young, too aggressive, absent from work after serial booze binges, and no good as a Father Christmas because of being a large-breasted woman. But being sacked for refusing to smoke is not something heavily indexed in the law reports.

The three sacked German employees have begun proceedings for unfair dismissal. Mr Jensen, however, seemed resolute. He noted that, among the deficiencies of the problematic non-smokers, was their tendency to "distance themselves from the smokers at social events", something especially irksome, he said, as "it didn't build any team spirit".

A relaxed beginning and abrupt end

Unlike a divorce, an annulment is an unusual way to end a marriage. Legally, it's a declaration that the marriage was never valid. But even in the unusual world of annulments, one granted by an appeal court in Italy in 2008 is extraordinary.

After a legal battle lasting over 10 years, an Italian woman had her marriage annulled because her husband smoked cannabis on their wedding night.

That evening, in their bedroom, when her husband said something to the effect of "now let us relax", among the things she was expecting him to do was decidedly not to roll a large joint. The woman, who is from a deeply traditional Italian family in Campagna, asked for a divorce immediately.

Following a detailed jurisprudential consultation with an ecclesiastical tribunal, the Appeal Court of Salerno, near Naples, has annulled the marriage. The woman had testified that she was outraged when he rolled the joint as, before the marriage, he had specifically denied ever smoking cannabis. The ecclesiastical tribunal had given an opinion that that the marriage was invalid because the man lied to his future wife about a material fact.

In her judgment, Angelo Rossi, president of the Appeal Court of Salerno, said, "The woman was a girl who grew up in a very conservative family and wanted a husband who was honest".

In England, some lawyers have done some deviant things on their wedding nights but have got away with it, especially if it involved hard work rather than enhanced relaxation. George Hill, a barrister who died in 1880, was a famously diligent advocate. He was a Serjeant (a distinguished barrister), who, because of his deeply detailed arguments was known to his chums as Serjeant Labyrinth. He had to be summoned from his desk to attend his own wedding ceremony after the church bells started ringing. That evening he went to his Temple chambers where he stayed reading cases until dawn. What Anna Barbara, his wife, thought of her wedding night isn't recorded.

A magistrate not on chill pills

Sentencing a young woman at the magistrates' court in Port Adelaide, Australia, in 2003, the magistrate said:

You're a druggie and you'll die in the gutter. That's your choice … I don't believe in that social worker crap. You abuse your mother and cause her pain. You can choose to be who you are. You can go to work. Seven million of us do it whilst 14 million like you sit at home watching *Days of Our Lives* smoking your crack pipes and using needles and I'm sick of you sucking us dry.

The magistrate then inveighed against certain taxes, and concluded "It's your choice to be a junkie and die in the gutter. No one gives a shit, but you're going to kill that woman who is your mother, damn you to death". He then gave the woman a prison sentence, apparently unaware that that was unlawful in the particular type of case in question. Allowing the defendant's appeal, Justice Perry eloquently condemned the delinquent magistrate saying that words like his reported remarks "have a corrosive effect upon public confidence in the functioning of the courts and in the administration of justice".

Not all at sea

The wonderfully titled *The King v Forty Nine Casks of Brandy* (1836) concerned an event in which 55 casks of brandy came ashore on the south coast near Poole in Dorset. The case concerned a dispute between the estate of William Bankes, a local property owner, and the King (in his office of Admiralty) as to who had the best title to the goods. The relevant area of law contains many fine distinctions. For example, to constitute "wreck of the sea", and so be subject to one set of rules, the goods must have touched the ground, though they need not have been left dry. Goods on the high seas, though below the low water mark, if they have not touched the ground are "droits" like flotsam and jetsam. Forty nine of the 55 casks had been taken to the Custom House at Weymouth. These were divided into categories according to where on the tide mark they had be seized, and assigned by the court, variously to the King and the estate of Bankes (who owned the nearby Corfe Castle), according to the rules. It is not recorded how the litigants celebrated their gains.

Salad days

Under English law, it is not a specific offence to position lettuce in your nose. Neither can you be punished for spitting out a chewed lettuce leaf – at least, not in most circumstances. If, however, you are a sandwich-bar worker and you commit those acts with lettuce that you then replace in the food tray from which customers select their sandwich ingredients, you are violating section 38 of the Public Order Act 1986, as Richard Benjamin Shannon discovered in 2009.

Shannon worked at the sandwich chain Subway in Brownhills, in the Midlands. His foray into providing secret salad dressing was filmed on a mobile phone by a friend and then posted on YouTube. Shannon was arrested by police after a later incident in which an irate woman, who recognised him from the YouTube film, went to the Subway where he worked, and hurled a chair at him.

The film of Shannon's conduct with the lettuce was viewed by the Bench at Walsall Magistrates' Court during his trial. Section 38 of the 1986 Act makes it an offence to contaminate or interfere with goods with the intention of "causing public alarm or anxiety". The law is exquisitely well-drafted so as not to allow any sly defences. It is even a crime to make it appear that goods have been contaminated or interfered with, or to place goods which appear to have been contaminated "in a place where goods of that description are consumed, used, sold or otherwise supplied ...".

The court, which could have sentenced Shannon to 6 months in prison, noted his remorse and guilty plea and ordered him to do 300 hours of unpaid work for the community. He will not though, we hope, be deployed to his local authority's 'meals on wheels' service. Still, at least he wasn't around in Henry VIII's reign when contaminating people's food was something for which the culprit was also punished 'in the community' but rather more severely. For poisoning the soup of the Bishop of Rochester in 1530, a man called Rose was publicly boiled to death in Smithfield in London.

The ingredients of fresh salad have played a limited but significant role in shaping some points of law. In the case of Shaun Kelly in 1992, the Court of Appeal looked at an appropriate sentence for someone who had robbed building societies using a cucumber. The vegetable was concealed in a plastic bag and brandished to look as though it were a gun. Kelly's sentence was 5 years.

In 2007, in the context of what the Police Federation described as pressure to meet government targets on arrests, a man was cautioned for being "in possession of an egg with intent to throw", and a child was arrested for flinging at another child a single slice of cucumber. *De minimis non curat lex* – the law doesn't concern itself with trifles – but salad is another matter.

A mere puff

In Italy, people caught in possession of marijuana have raised many diverse defences. "I was due to spend a long time alone up a mountain with a flock of sheep", broke new legal ground, however, when it was raised in 2009 by a shepherd as a defence in the Supreme Court of Cassation.

There was no precedent for the 'solo and ovine bound' defence, but it succeeded and the man was acquitted. So now the only crook on the mountain is the one in the shepherd's hand.

The 45-year-old man, identified in the law report as Giorogi D, had been caught in possession of 38 grams of marijuana during a random car check in Trentino-Alto Adige, in the far north of the country. Some of the drug was wrapped and some of it was in jars, mixed with tobacco.

The shepherd explained to police that he was about to spend a very long time alone with his sheep in the countryside and up a mountain as the flock was due to be migrated. The drug was to ease his hardship. None the less, he was prosecuted. The police took the view that, even though his story seemed true, the amount of marijuana he had was over the guideline for mere personal use. The trial court acquitted him and the prosecutor appealed.

The appeal court upheld the acquittal. It ruled that, when judging whether an amount of marijuana like that with which the shepherd was caught was for mere personal use, and therefore excusable, a court should examine how it was stored and all the circumstances. The trial court had been justified in acquitting the shepherd.

This is the first time sheep have helped exonerate a man from a criminal charge. In several cases, though, sheep have been the cause of men's legal downfall. These are generally incidents in which the culprit – intoning the sentiment 'ewe know I'm no good' – gets into a closer relationship with the animal than the law permits. In 2007, a man was arrested in south east London after someone was spotted in a decidedly non-agricultural relationship with a sheep – and his DNA was identified on a pair of abandoned jogging bottoms found at the scene.

No one wants a moment of intimate personal companionship to be witnessed, but some interruptions are worse than others. In 2002, a 23-year-old man was half-naked and engaged in such a liaison with a goat in a field called Paradise Allotments in the north east of England. To his horror, however, and perhaps to the goat's relief, a packed Hull-to-Bridlington train made a sudden unscheduled signal stop right beside them. Many of the aghast passengers made mobile calls to the police and the man was later arrested. At first he denied the encounter but was convicted after goat hairs were discovered in his underpants.

At Hull Crown Court, his lawyer pleaded for a non-custodial sentence saying his client would be prepared to go on a "victim awareness" course. A suitable course was not, though, offered by either the criminal justice system or the farmyard community so the man was sent from Paradise Allotments to Her Majesty's allotments for 6 months.

Out to lunch

Lavish food and drink feature in an 1894 case about local authority expenses. A local government board auditor had disallowed certain payments by the Dublin city corporation, one item being the cost of lunch for its members during the annual inspection of the local waterworks. The refusal to meet the cost at the expense of local taxpayers was upheld by the Irish Queen's Bench Division. Chief Justice O'Brien said the "sumptuous repast" for the local government members included:

> ... two dozen bottles of champagne, Ayala 1885 – a very good brand; one dozen Marcobrunn Hock – a very nice hock; one dozen Chateau Margaux – an excellent claret; one dozen bottles of fine old Dublin whiskey – the best whiskey that can be got; six bottles of Amontillado sherry – a stimulating sherry; and the ninth item is some more fine Dublin whiskey!

He stated "We do not say that the members of the Corporation are not to lunch. But we do say that they are not to do so at the expense of the citizens of Dublin".

Pieless in Vancouver

The Supreme Court of Canada heard a case in 2009 about an arrest for 'possession of a pie with unlawful intent'. Surreally, the pie didn't even exist – but the case has now become one of major constitutional importance in Canada.

The story started in 2002, when police said they believed that someone in Vancouver was going to throw a pie at Jean Chrétien, the Canadian Prime Minister. A judge later described the evidence for the plot as nothing more than "a third hand rumour". None the less, the police swung into action. The pie suspect was described by a radio dispatcher as 5 foot 9, with short dark hair and aged between 30 and 35. The police then arrested Cameron Ward – who is 6 foot with collar-length silver hair, and who was almost 45 at the time of the incident. Although Ward was clearly pie-less when stopped, acting on a suspicion that he might be "hiding pies", officers whisked him to jail where he was stripped and given a thorough personal search. No pies. He was then locked in a tiny cell for 4½ hours. Saying that they believed a pie might be hidden in Ward's car, officers didn't open the trunk but rather impounded his vehicle. This, though, was not Ward's first experience of unusual police conduct – he is a prominent lawyer often involved in litigating cases of alleged police misconduct.

One city officer continued to search for pie evidence for an astonishing 6 weeks after Ward's arrest, but none was found. Bakery policing was, however, executed more successfully by another force – the Royal Canadian Mounted Police. While Ward was being probed for pies, the Mounties in Vancouver (gun crime capital of Canada), arrested a man for possession of a piece of pineapple cake.

Ward sued the police, the city, and the provincial government for wrongful arrest, false imprisonment and negligence. He offered to settle the case in return for an apology but his offer was rejected. In court, a police officer who was asked whether she had found any evidence that Ward was guilty, replied bizarrely, "I did not come across any evidence that he was not". Ward won the case although the judgment swung on violations of the Canadian Charter of Rights and Freedoms, not on specifically illegal police conduct. He was awarded $10,000 damages and the appeal court upheld the award. The Supreme Court of Canada upheld that decision. In arriving at that decision, it had to consider in what circumstances damages should be awarded to a citizen whose constitutional rights have been infringed (like being kept in a cell too long), but where the authorities haven't broken any particular law – a point definitely not as easy as pie.

Chapter 4

JUDGES

Judges are a key part of any civilised society. With them around, we can live in a relatively peaceful way, safe in the knowledge that when there is any serious dispute between neighbours, citizens, or organisations, or whenever there is a criminal charge against anyone, the case will be presided over by a fair, dispassionate, independent, well-educated expert. Every day, millions of cases are heard over the world – and most of them are completed smoothly and without incident. But no branch of life is without its imperfections. And even the judiciary is fallible. "I think that a judge should be looked on rather as a sphinx than as a person" observed Judge HC Leon in 1975, "you shouldn't be able to imagine a judge having a bath". The trouble is that human fallibility among judges is periodically revealed in ways which encourage us to see them less as sphinxes and more as people who have inelegantly slipped over in the bath.

Flip justice

A judge who declares to litigants that he'll settle their child visitation dispute by flipping a coin, and who orders a woman to drop her trousers in court, is unlikely to enjoy a long and distinguished judicial career. And so it was with Judge James Michael Shull, who was removed from office in 2007 by the Virginia Supreme Court.

Shull admitted tossing a coin to determine which parent should have their child at Christmas. He said he was trying to encourage the parents to decide the issue themselves. The request for a woman to take down her trousers came in a case in which she was seeking a protective order against a partner who she said had stabbed her in the leg. The judge knew the woman had a history of mental problems, and said he wanted proof of her claim.

The Virginia Supreme Court noted that Shull had appeared before the Judicial Inquiry and Review Commission in 2004 for allegedly calling a teenager a "mama's boy" and a "wuss", and for advising a woman in court to marry her abusive boyfriend. That complaint was dismissed but Shull was asked to learn from the experience.

Worldwide, judges have been removed from office for some odd things, including smuggling whisky, and attending psychology classes as a student at a local university instead of presiding in court. But coin-tossing is rare. In an industrial injury case in England 1965, speaking about the way someone doing a judicial job should make his decisions, Lord Justice Diplock said "he must not spin a coin or consult an astrologer". And, so far, in the UK judges have done neither.

Judicial coin flipping, though, isn't unprecedented in America. "Is your client a gambling man?", Judge Alan Friess asked the lawyer of Jeffrey Jones at Manhattan Criminal Court in 1982. Jones had pleaded guilty to theft but had objected to a proposed 30-day jail sentence, saying 20 days would be fairer. The judge then asked a District Attorney for a 25 cent coin, and ordered the defendant to flip it and call. Jones called tails, won, and got his 20 days. But the New York State Commission on Judicial Conduct didn't want to gamble on Friess in future, and so flipped him from office.

What not to wear

In an English case in 1973, Mr Justice Megarry said the power of a court didn't depend on superficial things like the wig and gown of the judge. In a rural property dispute, he was planning to take the court to the site but to attend unrobed. He said there was no need to get hung up on "mere matters of attire".

Mere matters of attire, however, did become a problem for Judge Robert Somma. When the federal bankruptcy judge from Boston, Massachusetts, was arrested after a drink-driving incident in February 2008, he was taken from his car in clothes unusual even for a judge: a black cocktail dress, fishnet stockings, and high heels. With a proper detachment, the official police report, which doesn't cite the judge's dress, does note that he "had a difficult time locating his licence in his purse".

The judge pleaded guilty to the drink-driving offence and resigned. It would be contentious, though, if the resignation was connected with his dress preference. Certainly, for the guilty plea to a first offence misdemeanour such as the driving offence, the US Courts for the First Circuit would not demand a judge's resignation, although, of course, a court punishment would be imposed. No one was hurt in the incident in which the judge's vehicle knocked into a truck at a traffic light. The 63-year-old judge has a flawless judicial record and has attracted praise from lawyers and officials for his extensive knowledge and invariable fairness. The chief executive of the First Circuit described him as "an absolutely excellent judge".

Other judges have been known to have had some odd lawful private peccadilloes without having to resign. Even in exercising judicial functions, English judges have sometimes done so in unusual garb. Sir Lancelot Shadwell did so in a swimsuit in the Thames. Sir Samuel Evans gave judgment in a dressing-gown in his bedroom. In 1999, a judge with a broken leg refused to bow out of her duty to consider each argument of counsels' submissions. She showed true judicial dedication by handing down judgment in a multi-million pound trial from her hospital bed. Taking commitment and professionalism to soaring heights, with the approval of senior judges and the Lord Chancellor's Department, Judge Valerie Pearlman convened a 'virtual' courtroom by relaying images of her reading aloud her decision while so stricken.

The law in slow motion

"Everyone thought it was all done, and all of a sudden at the very end it was like 'whoa'", proclaimed Judge Evelyn Baker in St Louis, Missouri in 2008.

But she wasn't talking about the closing seconds of a basketball final or a movie with a twist just before the credits. She was talking about the case of *Senu-Oke v Modern Moving Systems Inc.*

The case was about a college teacher, Edward Senu-Oke, who had sued his moving company when his move from Wyoming to Wisconsin turned into a disaster. The case had been filed, however, 15 years earlier. The judge had found for the plaintiff in 2002 but hadn't issued a formal ruling. So the case just sat in a file for 6 years until it was discovered collecting dust in April 2008 when the judge was clearing out her office before her retirement.

After the judge had found in favour of the claimant in 2002, the defendant's lawyer was contacted but didn't reply. Then the judge's office forgot to chase the matter. Long delays followed. Today, that lawyer says he has never represented the defendants. The chronic delay was aggravated because the claimant's lawyer also forgot to follow up on the case. Between them, over 15 years, the judge and the lawyers on each side didn't give an entirely superb service in this case but they are all involved in the delayed judgment. And the judgment against the company was for, wait for it, "gross and reckless disregard for plaintiff's rights".

Then there were two more twists. On her last day in office, Judge Baker awarded the college instructor $1.5 million damages. Claimant grins widely. But the defendant has no money so the award is unlikely ever to be paid. Claimant gnashes teeth.

English judges haven't always been brisk in giving judgments. In 1823, Lord Eldon was pressed for his decision in *Collis v Nott*, which he had heard in 1817. He eventually confessed that he "had entirely forgotten it".

In 1998, Mr Justice Harman resigned after the Court of Appeal had given stinging criticism of his delay in giving a judgment. He was known as a rather maverick judge

– he once asked a female witness who'd said she'd like to be referred to with the title 'Ms': "I've always thought there were only three kinds of women: wives, whores and mistresses, which are you?". He ignored counsels' requests for judgments that were a long time coming. Then things came to a head when, following the case of a Lincolnshire farmer suing a firm of accountants, the judge didn't give the judgment for over 80 weeks.

During the absurd delay, the farmer's barrister got so frustrated that he considered taking out life insurance on the judge in case he died before giving judgment. The judge's attitude was a shocking case of judicial negligence. He eventually ruled, wrongly as it turned out, because he'd lost all his trial notes, that the farmer's claim should fail. And what sort of claim was it that the farmer had brought, and which the judge so confidently dismissed, with almost no papers and even less memory? Of course, it was a claim in negligence.

What price justice?

"Finally we are at a point where I think that justice is back on an even keel in Caddo Parish", declared US Attorney Donald Washington, in June 2009, after a couple of convicts had been jailed.

His sigh of relief came at the end of a racketeering case in Louisiana. Prior to sentencing two convicted men, District Judge Maurice Hicks had remanded them in custody because they were seen as otherwise likely to abscond. Unusually, however, for men facing sentences of up to 20 years for racketeering, both convicts were judges.

The men had been convicted of taking bribes to set low bail bonds or to remove court restrictions on defendants. A federal jury convicted District Judge Michael Walker of the state court, and Judge Vernon Claville of Caddo Parish juvenile court on one count each of racketeering. Claville was accused of taking bribes to remove court limitations from juveniles so they could get bail. Walker was accused of taking bribes to set bail bonds quickly, reduce them, recall arrest warrants or remove probation conditions. For just 3 sample months in 2007, 24 instances of pay-as-you-go justice were exposed. It sounds like the judges kept a credit card payphone in their chambers.

Judges have been removed from office for corruption in Britain, but not in modern times. In the 13th century, six judges were sacked for taking bribes. Later, Sir William De Thorpe, the Chief Justice was thrown off the Bench for taking bribes in 1350.

In the 16th century, referring to judges, Bishop Hugh Latimer said "they all love bribes. Bribery is a princely kind of thieving". Then, in 1620, Francis Bacon, the Lord Chancellor, pleaded guilty to 21 charges of bribery and corruption. He had accepted large bribes from litigants to get him to rule in their favour. He was fined £40,000 and sent to the Tower.

The known and reviled practice of bribing a judge can, though, be used to the advantage of a clever lawyer. This is an account I once heard some years ago from a Chief Justice of Lesotho. A client, whom I'll call Mr Crook, was a notorious character in the murky social territory between legitimate business and crime. The authorities eventually caught up with him and he'd been caught in the act. His lawyer was faced with a pretty much impossible task.

At the end of the trial, but before the verdict, the defence lawyer confided to his crooked client, "this doesn't look good I'm afraid, I think we'll have to just accept the verdict and appeal".

"Don't be a defeatist", said the client, "We'll just have to see what price we can get the judge for".

"No", said the lawyer, "there is no way that this judge can be bought. He is the apotheosis of integrity. He has absolute rectitude in all things. He is the embodiment of truth and justice and he would react with great repugnance to any improper offer".

"You think so?", the client asked, rhetorically.

"Don't do anything stupid", the lawyer advised.

The next day, the judge came into court and said he was throwing out the prosecution case against Mr Crook.

The prosecution lawyers sat wide-eyed and slack-jawed in disbelief.

The defendant beamed, winked at his lawyer, said, "I told you I'd fix it", and got up to go.

"I cannot believe it", said his lawyer, "but just tell me this – how did you do it?".

"Well", said the client, "last night I had delivered to the judge's front door six crates of the world's finest whisky".

"But this guy's completely incorruptible, I don't get it", said the defence lawyer.

"Yes, that's right, he *is* incorruptible", said the client, "but I had it delivered to the judge in the name of the prosecutor".

Judge this

"Justice is not a cloistered virtue", Lord Atkin said in 1936, so it can be strongly criticised provided its critics are "respectful".

Respect, though, was not what Judge Brad Thomas got when he went to discuss a judgment with someone. "Get out of my fucking office" he was told before being ejected. The outburst might have been easier to deal with, however, if the person shouting the abuse wasn't Judge Charles J Kahn Jr of the 1st District Court of Appeal in Florida.

In testimony at a preliminary hearing of the Judicial Qualifications Commission in 2008, Judge Kahn (formerly Chief Judge until deposed by his brethren) explained his loss of temper. Thomas had gone to see him to disagree with a judgment he'd given, and this riled Kahn, who said, "I had been on the court for 14 or 15 years and he had been on the court for a week or two".

The hearing had involved a jaw-dropping sequence of testimony in which senior judges accused each other of being "volatile" and "schizoid", of lying, having hotel sex with court employees, and of threatening behaviour. Evidently, an everyday tale of life on the judicial Bench and bed.

Don Brannon, court marshal for 27 years at the Florida courthouse, said he thought Kahn was unstable and he became worried when the judge seemed set to apply for a concealed weapons permit and a handgun. Anxiety deepened when two other judges decided to get guns. So Brannon arranged for extra police security at a judicial ceremony. Other evidence about Kahn involved stories of his affairs with female court staff, including liaisons with a clerk and photos of them in a South Florida hotel.

But it wasn't Judge Kahn who was on trial. For that, we need to swing 180 degrees to face one of his critics. That was Judge Michael E Allen, charged with "conduct unbecoming of a judge". It broke down like this. Judge Kahn had allowed the appeal of a politician convicted of corruption. But the judge's former law partner was close to the reprieved politician, so it looked like Kahn might not have been neutral. Judge Allen was charged with "conduct unbecoming" after he wrote an opinion critical of Kahn for sitting in the case.

The evidence of up to 15 senior judges was scheduled as relevant to the full hearing. Acrimonious threats among them to sue and complain abounded. Presumably any judge entering the hearing with a gavel in his hand would be required to disarm.

Taming the testifiers

"I usually deal with financial fraud and company law", said Judge Brigitte Koppenhoefer, "this was all just so ridiculous I couldn't help it". She was referring to a case in Düsseldorf, Germany, involving a dispute between two feuding neighbours that became so daft she had to vacate the Bench.

Judge Koppenhoefer, who normally presides in major cases involving millions of euros, is accomplished in dealing with fraught disputes in a cool, dignified manner but she was reduced to unguarded giggles when the nature of the neighbour quarrel she was hearing unfolded in her court in 2008.

She had listened impassively for a few minutes to how the embattled neighbours had sent each other filth-filled letters and engaged in egg fights. But there's only so long that a judicial lower lip can be bitten to prevent laughter. When the two litigants began referring to each other in court in very loud and serious tones as "donkey face" and "smelly bottom" the judge halted the proceedings, rose, and went out the judge's door to give vent to her laughter in a private place. Following a short break she re-entered the court and dismissed the case.

Trials involving animated witnesses haven't always been contained by conventional methods. In 1969, David Dellinger, a leading American antiwar campaigner, and seven others were put on trial in Chicago for political conspiracy. They had organised peace protests against the Vietnam war. After one of the defendants, Bobby Seale, made repeated interruptions to the trial, Judge Julius J Hoffman ordered him to be bound and gagged in the courtroom. The following morning, Seale was carried into the court on a chair with his limbs strapped to it and with a large gag covering most of his face. All he could do was writhe and groan. Quite how getting medieval on a defendant was supposed to enhance justice wasn't made clear.

Some judges, though, have vowed to deal with disruption in court by even more direct means. In a case from Syracuse, New York, recounted from the court transcript by Charles M Sevilla in 1993, the judge had been listening to a dispute about sustained illegal parking in a handicapped zone. The litigant had become outspoken and things got a bit unruly. The judge explained his ruling and then asked the litigant whether it was clear. The litigant said it was. The judge then opted to eliminate any possibility of doubt:

Judge: Otherwise, if you want to park in a handicapped spot, I will come over and break your leg for you so you so you can use it legally.

Litigant: Is that a threat, sir?

Judge: Next time you come in this court and make that kind of noise, you son-of-a-bitch, I will send you to jail, you got it?

Litigant: Yes.

Judge: Keep that mouth of yours shut or I will come in there myself and strangle you, you bastard. Get out of here.

So, don't think that all judges reach for an old Latin phrase to nail a point.

Sticky ending

In a case from Ohio in 2009, Judge Stephen Belden decided that a defendant in a robbery case was offending the dignity of the court by talking too much. The judge, however, chose an unorthodox way to establish decorum: he ordered the defendant's mouth to be sealed with duct tape. That is a court exercise you won't find on the judicial training syllabus.

The defendant, Harry Brown, was appearing in a preliminary hearing charged with theft from a Wal-mart store. He objected to his state-appointed defence attorney and fell into an argument with the judge about his options. They disputed legal points for about 3 minutes. The judge told Brown that the American constitution did require that an attorney be provided free of charge if he couldn't afford one but it did not have to be an attorney the defendant liked. He said Brown was not entitled to a lawyer with whom he had "a warm and fuzzy relationship".

Brown continued to dispute the quality of the service he had received from his court-appointed lawyer and spoke over the judge. Although Brown was composed and did not raise his voice, the judge then declared that if there were any further interruptions he was going to get some duct tape and order the bailiff to stick it over Brown's mouth. Brown continued politely to object to the way he was being treated, prompting this unique utterance in the records of judicial proceedings:

Judge: All right, duct tape. Duct tape the defendant.

Brown was then officially gagged with tape. Why the Bench had a ready supply of duct tape among law reports and legal paraphernalia was left unexplained. After a while Brown was given another chance and the tape was removed subject, the judge said, to him not reverting to his "disrespectful ways".

"I am not being disrespectful, Your Honour, I think you're being more disrespectful to me", Brown replied, as the bailiff scrunched the strip of used duct tape implanted with the defendant's epilated facial hair. Taking Brown's words as a final impertinence, the judge gave an immediate ruling that there was a 'probable cause' for a full trial, and had him unceremoniously taken away.

While interrupting a judge can result in pain, interruptions *by* a judge can be equally problematic. In an Old Bailey case in 1943, a couple of prostitutes were accused of robbing a client. Quashing their convictions, the Court of Appeal noted the trial judge had been excessive in his interruptions, cutting in to the defendants' testimony with his own points 495 times. But that record was broken in a 1951 case in which counsel for both sides complained about a judge in Liverpool who had interrupted testimony 587 times. Genteelly, though, they sought a remedy from the Court of Appeal not duct tape.

From the frying pan to fired

District Judge Elizabeth Halverson appeared, in November 2008, before the Nevada Commission on Judicial Discipline, charged with 14 counts of judicial misconduct.

Her attorney conceded that "she is not perfect". After considering the evidence, however, the commission went a little further. It found her to be paranoid, mercurial, boorish, Quixotic, combative, disrespectful, dismal, and a deliberate liar. It deposed her from the Bench and barred her from judicial office for life.

Testimony against her came from many sources but the evidence of her bailiff was especially damning. Breaking down in the witness box, he choked, "I can't stand what she did to me". He testified how she made him pick dirt off her judicial robes, cuddled him when he chauffeured her to judicial events, and periodically instructed him to take off her shoes and rub her feet.

He also testified that he had often heard the judge on the phone screaming at her husband with phrases such as, "I am sick of your ass. Why don't you do what the fuck I tell you?". He testified that she had once asked him to shoot her husband, saying it would be okay as she would be able to dispose of the body.

During the disciplinary case, the hearing had to be suspended when Judge Halverson was rushed to hospital from home one night suffering from severe injuries after her husband smashed her head with a frying pan. A charge of attempted murder against her husband was dropped as he pleaded guilty to assault with a deadly weapon. He will serve up to 10 years in prison.

Halverson's defence at the resumed misconduct hearing wasn't a *tour de force*. She had a row with the first lawyers she hired. She fired them, and then sued the Judicial Discipline Commission. That, though, didn't avert her disciplinary case. At the hearing, eight of her witnesses did not arrive to give testimony, she blamed all her judicial mistakes on lawyers, and she sought to explain the foot massages as something her bailiff did out of the goodness of his heart.

The full published findings against Halverson included that she fell asleep in front of juries, yelled profanities, had improper contact with jurors, blamed others for her own inadequacies, had improper contact with the media, breached court security by hiring her own private security personnel, lied under oath, and had her bailiff massage "her feet, neck and shoulders, or some combination of those body parts". She was also found to have repeatedly referred to members of the court staff as "bitches" and "dumb-fucks".

English judges have occasionally been injudicious. Historically, the punishment for judicial misconduct was more than losing your post and pension. There is evidence that King Alfred hanged 44 judges in a single year for having "vexed the people". Mr Justice Charles, who sat in the 1940s, was described by a law lord as a vulgar, unjust, decrepit old man who belched from beer and was a blot on the administration of justice.

The oddest cases of judicial intemperance, though, come from America. In one, a Los Angeles judge, interceding in a bitter exchange between two lawyers, said that, if they continued, he would descend from the Bench and kick them in the genitals. He then explained how worthless he thought they were by saying, "I have shot and killed better men than both of you".

Wyrd case

A lawyer who advises a client to sue a trio of judges is asking for trouble. And trouble is what came to face the Canadian advocate, Kimberly Townley-Smith.

In 2005, Ms Townley-Smith represented the group Wyrd Sisters in a $40 million action against Warner Bros. The folk group from Winnipeg alleged that the company, which makes the Harry Potter films, had appropriated their name for Weird Sisters, a group featured in *Harry Potter and the Goblet of Fire*. The action failed as the court decided that the folk group was unlikely to be confused with the differently spelt rock group in the film.

Dissatisfied, Townley-Smith then targeted three judges involved in the case and sued them for conspiracy, alleging they'd all been involved in a sinister "dysfunction" against her client. She demanded $21 million for conspiracy, fraud, misrepresentation, abuse of process, and abuse of public office. She accused the judges of skulduggery, lying, and case-fixing. Those are accusations you wouldn't want to be making against judges without a watertight case – but Ms Townley-Smith's case was a sieve.

In rejecting the conspiracy claim, Mr Justice Hackland, sitting in the Ontario Supreme Court in 2008, ruled that the case against the judges was a "scurrilous attack on the administration of justice by a member of the Bar". The standard rule giving judges immunity from being sued for their court decisions was enough to defeat the Wyrd Sisters in this case.

Mr Justice Hackland said that, while any advocate is allowed to put the case of their client "fearlessly, resolutely and honourably", Townley-Smith had strayed into "forbidden ground" by improperly advancing her own opinions and having an improper purpose. She also tried to act as both a witness and counsel in the same case. She was ordered to appear before the court to show good cause why she shouldn't be held personally liable for the costs of the case.

Other jurisdictions have the same rule giving judges immunity against being sued for their judicial work. In a Nigerian case in 1970, Justice Atake took exception to the conduct of a barrister appearing before him. Believing he'd been accused by the barrister of fumbling the law, the judge got very defensive. He told the court how clever he was, saying he'd finished his legal course in only 18 months, and reassured everyone that "many people considered me a brilliant student". When the barrister tried to defend himself, the judge boomed out, "Sit down, stupid". The judge convicted the barrister for contempt and had him detained. The conviction was eventually set aside but the barrister's subsequent civil action against the judge failed – on the judicial immunity principle.

The law has occasionally allowed claimants some limited litigation victories against those on the Bench, but the compensation hasn't been high. In 1986, Lapido Solanke stopped paying a maintenance order to his ex-wife and was imprisoned for 42 days by magistrates. It turned out that the imprisonment was unlawful because the maintenance order had never been registered with the magistrates' court. After his release from jail, Solanke sued the magistrates for £1.4 million. Applying legislation that then existed, however, the Court of Appeal limited his compensation to the rather lower sum of one penny.

Roo the day in court

Three men who attended court in Singapore wearing T-shirts that pictured a kangaroo dressed as a judge, in November 2008, were sentenced to jail for contempt of court.

A "kangaroo court" is an unfair tribunal that disregards proper procedure. The term originated in the 1849 Californian gold rush (to which many Australians had travelled), and referred to claims tribunals that leapt over many of the normal stages of due process in order to land on a preferred verdict.

The Singaporean men's T-shirt protest was prosecuted as a form of contempt known as 'scandalising the judiciary'. The prosecutor asked for custodial sentences. He said an allegation that a court is a kangaroo court was the worst insult that can be levelled at the judicial system.

The men were members of the opposition Singapore Democratic Party (SDP), which had been found liable for defaming the Prime Minister and a government minister. Wearing the judicial kangaroo shirts, they went to a hearing in the Supreme Court in May 2008, at which the judge was to set the defamation damages payable by the SDP.

At their subsequent contempt trial, they were given an opportunity to apologise for their insinuation and to withdraw it. They declined to do so. They told the court that, on their analysis, the T-shirt they'd worn to the defamation hearing could not amount to contempt and that its message was fair criticism. One of the defendants told the judge the meaning of the T-shirt was to express a hope that the quality of justice would be improved. He said, politely, that by wearing the shirt, he'd hoped to identify "weaknesses in the system".

The court disagreed. One defendant, a senior officer of the SDP, was given a 15-day jail sentence; the others got 7 days. Each man was also ordered to pay $5,000 to the prosecutor's office.

Across the world, all sorts of conduct has been punished under the law against scandalising a court or contempt "in the face of the court". Convicts have included people who have sung songs at the judge, distributed leaflets in court, wolf-whistled at a juror, shouted insults, and someone who gradually stripped off to lie naked on a courtroom bench.

The person, though, who should have been least surprised to have spent time in jail for scandalising the court was the editor of the *Oriental Daily News* in Hong Kong in 1999. His paper had published articles that severely criticised the integrity of several judges but, very resentful of the Bench, he then went a step further. He staged a 3-day paparazzi campaign in which he commissioned a horde of photographers to hound and monitor the daily activity of a Court of Appeal judge in order to "teach him a lesson". The Court of Appeal responded by reversing the educational process: it sentenced the editor to 120 days in jail.

Taking the urine

In Tennessee, a judge is legally required to be "patient, dignified and courteous" with everyone in court. He is also required, not unreasonably, "to respect and comply with the law". But not all judges do comply.

The Supreme Court of Tennessee disciplined Judge Durwood Moore in 2009 for unlawful judicial conduct. Presiding in court one day, the judge happened to glance at Benjamin Marchant, a friend of someone who had court business. Marchant was not a witness, just a spectator. Yet, after observing him, the judge, apparently believing himself to have the power of a medieval monarch, ordered court officers to seize Marchant, get a urine sample from him, and have it tested for drugs. The sample came back negative. The judge was found guilty of acting unlawfully and undermining public confidence in the administration of justice. Judge Dredd declared "I am the law" but Judge Moore did not get away with it. He was given public censure, the harshest form discipline short of being recommended for removal from office. It was clearly his last chance. Remarkably, though, on the same day that the Court of the Judiciary censured Moore for the drugs test travesty, it also ruled against him in another case. He had wrongly and irascibly refused a lawyer's request to allow someone else to present a document. He had then "used profanity" to the lawyer on the phone, threatening him with a contempt finding if he didn't return to court to present the document himself.

Bizarre instances of unlawful judicial cussedness in British trials (later overturned on appeal) include an English judge who fined a man for accidentally walking into court in Surrey wearing his hat, and a Scottish judge who fined a man for simply shaking his head while the prosecutor was summing up. The award for Most Unjudicial Petulance, though, goes to a judge in a 1968 criminal trial in London. During defence counsel's final address to the jury, the judge kept sighing in despair. Several times he loudly exclaimed "Oh God". Finally, he laid his head across his arms and made groaning noises. Just as bizarrely, though, the appeal court upheld the conviction of the defendant in that case saying the trial judge's conduct wouldn't have prejudiced the jury.

Lecture this

Faced with a tough legal challenge, a law academic should be able to strip away anything superficial, and quickly get to the bottom of the matter.

Megumi Ogawa, a lecturer in law, did that unconventionally, though, when representing herself in an Australian trial in 2009. Unimpressed by the prosecution's case against her, she lowered her trousers and bared her buttocks at the judge. She was given a predictably poor mark, and jailed for 4 months for contempt at Brisbane District Court.

Ogawa, who had lectured in law at the Southern Cross University in Lismore, New South Wales, was on trial for two counts of using a carriage service (the telephone system or internet) to harass and to threaten to kill two court officials. During a long conflict with the court system, she had sent 83 emails and made 176 calls to court staff.

During the preliminary proceedings, Ogawa sacked a series of lawyers before deciding to represent herself. Then, during the trial, apart from her mooning, she was forcibly removed from the court several times for sustained high-pitched screaming, making statements calculated to bring the justice system into disrepute, and violent wrestling with security officers. Her law lectures must have been lively events.

She was convicted of the harassment and death threat charges and sentenced to 6 months in jail, in addition to the 4 months for her contempt. She had to be held down in the dock by three security officers when being told by the judge of her sentence.

Using a bottom as a gesture of contempt has historically been treated with varying degrees of severity. In 1615, a Plymouth magistrate, expressed his opinion about the mayor by posturing his bottom "in an inhuman and uncivil manner" at the dignitary, and saying to him, "come and kiss". But a court decided that wasn't enough to warrant the magistrate being removed from office.

The award for most impassive unclothed contempt goes jointly to Messrs Gohoho and Gough. After being ordered to pay £50 into court as a security payment in 1964 for a forthcoming action, Mr Moses Gohoho manifested his despair in the High Court by removing his trousers and underpants and lying on the court bench in front of the judges with the implicit message: security this. In 2005, in Scotland, Stephen Gough was arrested and prosecuted for a breach of the peace for walking naked on the outskirts of Edinburgh. He later attended court to face the charge naked. When he was found to be in contempt for being undressed in court, he appealed, and his lawyer argued that appearing naked in a law court was a "fundamental human right". The Court of Appeal disagreed and ruled that presenting your genitals to a judge in a law court was a fundamental human wrong.

Chapter 5

DEATH AND VIOLENCE

The English lawyer Herbert Hart wrote that as a core part of our legal system we need rules against violence to stop society becoming a "suicide club". Most legal systems began from rules of elemental importance such as "thou shalt not kill". Today, there are thousands of rules controlling every conceivable type of violence including threats and verbal assaults. Oliver Wendell Holmes, the distinguished American judge wrote that "The right to swing my fist ends where the other man's nose begins". Happily, he spent his time swinging only his pen in the composition of judgments but many others across the world have not heeded his principle and some bizarre cases of violence have ended up in court.

Filing for anger

Justin Boudin, 27, was told to expect a sentence of 120 days in jail for the assault to which he pleaded guilty, in March 2008, at Ramsey County District Court in St Paul, Minnesota.

Falling into an argument with a 59-year-old woman at a bus stop, he became very aggressive and shouted abuse at her. When she nervously took out her phone to call the police, Mr Boudin sought to resolve the situation by hitting her in the face.

Then, when a 63-year-old man intervened and tried to restrain him, the enraged Boudin, who was holding a hard document file, moved into phase two of his conflict resolution strategy. He smashed the man with the file, and then left the bus stop. Clearly, rage had got the better of Boudin as he abandoned the file at roadside. Witnesses said he yelled, "Why don't you show me some respect?".

As the file bore his name, it didn't take police long to trace him. The file had been a cruel weapon because of the heavy copious notes it contained. In what subject had Boudin been so industrious? It was his homework file for the anger management course to which he was travelling when he became infuriated.

Clearly, Mr Boudin will have to put his homework to better use if he is to steer clear of the courts again.

This is not the first case in which anger has got the better of someone who was supposed to be demonstrating something else. In 2001, at the Royal Courts in London, Andy Covey was representing himself in a case before Lord Woolf, the Lord Chief Justice. As the case began, Mr Covey quickly stripped to his underpants then began to make his submissions. A security officer was called but before Mr Covey could be ejected, he took off his underpants and screamed a lewd comment at the Bench. He then shouted furious abuse at the Lord Chief Justice, and threw a jug of water over him. The Lord Chief showed noble restraint, imposing no punishment. He simply dismissed the case. So Mr Covey never got the chance to finish his representation. The reason he'd been in court in the first place was to persuade the judge to overturn an earlier ban on him bringing any more actions as he'd been legally classified as a "vexatious litigant".

In the frame

"Give me all the money from the safe or I am going to batter you", shouted Kevin Staples, waving a stick as he tried to rob the Bottoms Up liquor store in Bournemouth, Dorset in 2008.

But Mr Staples would not be a good candidate for any criminal team like Ocean's 11. The shop assistant at whom he made these threats wasn't unduly alarmed because Mr Staples suffers from severe arthritis, a ruined hip, and back problems – and he walks with a Zimmer frame.

When the shop assistant said that he had no access to the safe, Staples begrudgingly changed his tack and said "give me some fags then".

But two days after his Bottoms Up plan went bottom up, he attempted another robbery, this time at a shop called Past Times in Crawley, West Sussex. On this occasion, he brandished a 12-inch bread knife at a shop worker and barked "get the money out".

At his trial for robbery, attempted robbery, and assault, Bournemouth Crown Court heard that he tried to lunge over the counter. When staff shouted at him, he put his knife back into a bag on his Zimmer frame and left the store as quickly as he could – which was very slowly – only stopping outside to punch a security guard.

He later said he committed the crimes after voices had urged him to do so. He was sentenced to a minimum of 4 years' imprisonment.

Unsuccessful robberies are not uncommon. When Marcus Brewster, 21, and his 16 year-old accomplice entered a Domino's Pizza in Cincinnati, Ohio, in June 2008, they showed they were armed. This was followed by some remark like the famed one in the opening scene of *Pulp Fiction*: "Everybody be cool, this is a robbery". In fact, things were about to get a lot cooler for them than they realised. In trying to make a quick escape, they opened a door at the rear of the pizza parlour, ran through it, and slammed it shut behind them. It wasn't, though, into sunshine and freedom that they ran – but into the pizza freezer room where they were kept until the police arrived.

The prize, however, for the most quickly caught robber goes to Clive Bunyan. In 1970, Mr Bunyan raided the village store in Cayton, Yorkshire. He had burst into the shop carrying an imitation gun and wearing a motorcycle crash helmet. He escaped with £157 but police were able to track him down swiftly from a single clue appearing in capital letters on the front of his crash helmet: CLIVE BUNYAN.

Eating people is wrong

In a case in 1971, Lord Denning observed that "if hunger were once allowed to be an excuse for stealing, it would open a door through which all kinds of lawlessness and disorder would pass". That argument applies with even greater force where the law wants to stop people with a hunger for another sort of crime: cannibalism.

In 2003, Armin Meiwes was prosecuted in Germany for cannibalism even though his victim, Bernd Brandes, apparently volunteered to be Meiwes's dinner after seeing an internet advert for willing victims. Meiwes said: "There are hundreds and thousands of people out there who want to be eaten". He was convicted and jailed for manslaughter.

Cannibalism has been considered by the English courts. In a notorious case heard by Baron Huddleston in November 1884, Captain Thomas Dudley and Edwin Stephens were prosecuted for the murder of a cabin boy, Richard Parker. After the yacht they were sailing from Southampton to Sydney capsized, they found themselves on a dinghy 1,600 miles from shore. After 20 days adrift they killed Parker, eating his liver and drinking his blood. They were rescued 4 days later by a German vessel and were convicted of murder at Exeter Assizes, although their death sentences were later commuted to 6 months' imprisonment without hard labour. Their defence of "necessity" was rejected. No killing of an innocent person was permissible by a citizen except in self-defence against an assailant. Lord Coleridge said that "to preserve one's life is generally speaking a duty, but it may be the plainest and highest duty to sacrifice it".

In the UK, a case like that of Meiwes would be treated as murder because the victim's consent isn't a defence to a serious crime. The principle of individual autonomy is trumped by the principle of what is "needed in the public interest". The cases, however, have been a little fraught when a sexual element is present, and the rulings are not clear and consistent. In 1994 the House of Lords considered the case of five men who had been convicted of various assaults on each other in the course of voluntary sado-masochistic sex. The conduct, including branding and bloodletting, was ruled to be criminal by three of the five lords hearing the appeal. Some violence against the person is lawful, for example ritual circumcision, tattooing, ear-piercing and boxing, but sexual violence was ruled to be unlawful. According to three law lords, the criminality of such violence could not be negated by the consent of the victims – a principle endorsed by the European Court of Human Rights as "necessary in a democratic society".

In 1996, however, the Court of Appeal considered violence in the context of a marriage in which, with the wife's consent, the husband used a hot knife to burn his initials on her bottom. His conviction at Doncaster Crown Court for assault was quashed and the Court of Appeal declared that the branding was legally indistinguishable from lawful tattooing. The court said that it was not in the public interest to criminalise "consensual activity between husband and wife, in the privacy of the matrimonial home".

Just not cricket

Whether misconduct in sport is bad enough to be criminal depends on all the circumstances. The law says you need to consider "the type of the sport, the level at which it is played, the nature of the act, the degree of force used, the extent of the risk of injury, [and] the state of mind of the defendant".

In 2004, a Cambridgeshire village cricket match between Elsworth and Cambridge St Giles descended into something that was decidedly not cricket.

Joshua Fay, 14, was hurt after being attacked by a batsman he had just bowled out. He claimed that Michael Butt, 32, hit him with his bat and repeatedly punched him seconds after he had celebrated Butt's dismissal. Cambridge Crown Court was told that Butt thought that Fay had called him a "tosser" under his breath.

Joshua's father, Edward Fay, was hit by Butt after striding on to the field to defend his son. Joshua said of Butt: "He completely lost it. Something must have happened to him before. He just flipped".

Butt was acquitted of affray but admitted the assault on Joshua and was sentenced to 175 hours' community work and ordered to pay £200 compensation. "Somebody once said that the Battle of Waterloo was won on the playing fields of Eton", Judge Gareth Hawkesworth noted when giving sentence. "It is a saying", he continued, "which I have never fully understood because as far as I am concerned war has no place on the playing field and it had no place here".

Bottoms up

The identity of an alleged bank robber in a German case in 2008 depended on the reliability of testimony about the size of her bottom. A witness said the culprit had an unusually large backside. So, a variant on the common question, "Does my bottom look big in this?" became the key evidence issue in the case: "Does my bottom look big in this bank queue?".

A bank in Norf in western Germany had been robbed at gunpoint and the robber had escaped with €15,000. The main clue police had to work on was that witnesses had reported the suspect was a woman with "a very large backside" and "powerful thighs".

Then, some weeks later, one of those witnesses was standing in a queue in the same bank when he noticed what he thought was the same backside. He said he was sure because he would "never forget anything that big". He called the police and the suspect, 26-year-old Sandra Meiser, was arrested and found to be in possession of a ski mask and a handgun. She was suspected of being about to rob the same bank again. She was charged with firearms offences and attempted robbery, standing trial in September 2008.

The size of a bottom was once relevant to the outcome of an English case but the court was not very enthusiastic about the prospect of meticulously evaluating the evidence. In 1983, the television critic Nina Myskow had slated the performance of the actress Charlotte Cornwell in a series called *No Excuses*. The review had said, among other things, "her bum is too big". The actress sued. Counsel for the critic suggested that the courts were "not the place to deal with someone's sense of grievance that another person has been rude in print about their bottom", but the court disagreed. The case ploughed on and after a retrial Ms Cornwell eventually won £11,500 in damages.

In the German case, the mistake allegedly made by Ms Meiser is that, while being easily identifiable, she tried to rob the same bank twice. Bank robbers, however, have made worse mistakes than that. In 1975, a Scottish court heard that three men intent on robbery had charged into the Royal Bank of Scotland at Rothesay but had got stuck in the revolving doors. They had to be helped free by the staff, after which they sheepishly left the building. Moments later they rushed back in, declared they were robbing the bank, and demanded £5,000 cash but got no reaction other than laughter from the head cashier. One of the robbers then jumped over the counter in a rage but crashed to the floor clutching his ankle. Seeing that, the other two tried to make their getaway but, once again, got trapped in the revolving doors.

A very serious mistake

Being a back-stabber isn't necessarily a bar to becoming a lawyer. It is occasionally said to be an advantage in some law firms. Shooting people in the back, however, is a different matter – even cynics agree that is incompatible with being a good lawyer.

In 2009, the Law Society of Upper Canada heard the case of a man who argued that the fact that he shot someone in the back while he was hijacking a plane should not prevent him from being a lawyer. He is applying for a licence to practise law.

In 1984, Parminder Singh Saini shot at several people on board an Air India flight carrying 264 people. Twenty minutes into the flight, he put a gun to the head of a flight attendant and fired. The attendant survived but there was a predictable reaction among passengers. Risking the plane's destruction, and the consequential carnage,

Saina then fired several more shots. One of his shots hit a crew member in the back. Other passengers were stabbed by members of Saini's terrorist squad. He seized control of the aircraft and forced it to land in Pakistan where everyone was told to say their final prayers as the plane was going to be blown up. Saini was eventually arrested and sentenced to death. His sentenced was then commuted to life imprisonment in Pakistan but he was released after 10 years on condition that he left the country. He did so and gained entry to Canada by lying and then qualified as a lawyer.

During his 'fitness to practise' hearing in 2009, Saini engaged his capacity for legal analysis. Referring to his act of terrorism he conceded "I had no legitimate right to do that". Well, that is one way of putting it, certainly. He went on to explain that he also understood the underlying reason why shooting people on a plane in mid-flight should be avoided: "It's not legal". Clearly, he had done his reading in law school. Referring to the mid-air terrorism and shooting people as "a very serious mistake", Saini's lawyer told the Law Society tribunal he should be given the right to practise law in Canada.

Barristers have been convicted of various acts of aggression ranging from biting a policeman to attacking a barber with a fencing sabre. Acts of violence, though, don't necessarily ruin a legal career. In 1900, an English barrister from Liverpool was on a tram when a man boarded it and jostled a female passenger. The barrister went over and punched the man in the face so hard he sent him flying on to the kerb where he cracked his head and was killed instantly. The barrister fled the scene and left England on a vessel sailing to the Mediterranean. He lived in Malta for a while then, being caught in bed with another man's wife, smashed a chamber-pot over the husband's head and fled the scene again. He was never charged for the killing or the assault but went on to have a distinguished career at the Bar as FE Smith and later became Lord Chancellor.

Law v Voodoo

Defendants have sometimes defiantly given the finger to a court that was about to condemn them – but Remi Fakorede went further.

Facing conviction in a £1m state benefits fraud case in London, Fakorede suddenly pulled out a tissue containing three small severed fingers and waved them to the court. Following gasps and an emotional reaction among jurors, the case was temporarily halted.

Fakorede said the fingers were from her baby daughter. She claimed they had fallen off as the result of a Voodoo man's curse and that she'd been forced to commit a tax credit fraud under threat from the same demonic Voodoo man and from a relative known as Auntie Marian. As defences go, that is an unusual one.

The 46-year old defendant ran the scam for 5 years during which time she submitted false claims for state benefits on behalf of various imaginary families and children. She submitted 39 false claims for phantom children. She recruited her elder daughter to launder £925,933 garnered from the scheme. The authorities were alerted to the criminal enterprise after Fakorede made claims for non-existent childcare. The suspicions of officers were confirmed after all the relevant regular payments were terminated but none of the named beneficiaries complained.

After the finger incident in court, DNA tests demonstrated that the digits were indeed from Fakorede's baby daughter. The child had evidently suffered from gangrene after kidney failure. Fakorede, who was shown to have lied consistently in getting the £925,933, ran a hairdressing salon and owned two properties in East London. She was also in receipt of a £40,000 annual income from Nigeria.

In July 2008, at Southwark Crown Court, Judge Jacqueline Beech said in sentencing Fakorede "I find you to be a thoroughly dishonest woman. Your conduct in court was a barefaced attempt to manipulate the jury". She was sentenced to 5 years' imprisonment.

This was not the first time fingers detached from a body have appeared in an English court. In 1631, a condemned defendant in Salisbury expressed his displeasure with the court by throwing a large stone at Chief Justice Richardson. At that moment, though, the judge happened to slouch "in a lazie recklesse manner" and so the missile narrowly missed him, flying over his head. He later wryly observed "if I had been an upright judge, I had been slain".

But the judge's response to the defendant didn't involve sending the defendant on an anger management programme. The judge ordered the immediate amputation of the defendant's right hand. It was cut off in court and then fixed to the gibbet where the defendant was hanged.

Bitter sweet

In the UK, the law relating to pineapples is narrow. Until recent times, the rules only stipulated when a pineapple must be sold with its weight specified. A Scottish court decision has since confirmed that, legally, the fruit can be an agent of harm in an assault.

A former policewoman who was struck on the sternum by a flying pineapple during a disturbance was, in October 2008, awarded £3,000 damages.

Although £3,000 sounds just about reasonable for a pineapple attack, Tracey Ormsby, the claimant, originally submitted a wider claim for £1.5 million. She said she had suffered serious psychological injuries, including a major depressive disorder and agoraphobia after the attack by a mob at Govanhill Baths in Glasgow in 2001.

In October 2008, however, at the Court of Session in Edinburgh, Lord Malcolm doubted the extent of her mental injury following evidence that since the assault she had taken several foreign holidays, joined a gym, and acquired a new boyfriend after ending her previous relationship with a married officer. Her love life became relevant because the male officer accused her of threatening to send his wife compromising photos of him unless he agreed to give perjured evidence on Ormsby's behalf.

Ms Ormsby, of Strathclyde police, was ordered to attend a protest in 2001. The baths were to be closed, and a furious crowd had assembled to try to stop workmen from boarding up the premises. After violent disorder erupted, and missiles including the pineapple were thrown at the police, senior officers breached their duty of care to their staff by keeping them in a cordon after the risk of serious injury arose.

The court ruled that Ms Ormsby was entitled to an award for her minor physical injuries but rejected her claim for psychological injury. Lord Malcolm said he could not reconcile the Ms Ormsby he saw giving "robust, combative and feisty" testimony in the witness box with "the fearful and fragile person" described in some of the medical reports.

Flying fruit has rarely been of significance in English law though it did feature unexpectedly in one case. On 2 December 1938, the Court of Appeal ruled that a man who had hurled tomatoes at its judges had committed a gross contempt of court.

Frank Harrison, representing himself, had made an application for a new trial in a civil case which he had lost. When his argument was rejected by the appeal court, Harrison withdrew a number of tomatoes from his pocket and hurled them in a fusillade at Lords Justice Clauson and Goddard. Physically as well as mentally agile, though, the judges avoided all the shots.

Harrison was swiftly sentenced to 6 weeks' imprisonment. His final submission to the Bench wasn't ideally framed to improve his situation. Pulled away to the cells, he shouted "It is a pity I was not a better shot". But, 3 weeks later, his profuse apology was accepted and he was released for Christmas. To enjoy plum pudding, you must sometimes first eat humble pie.

Chapter 6

Pets and Animals

In a surreal James Thurber cartoon published in 1935, a judge is looking over the Bench into the well of court as an attorney holds on to a large kangaroo and points to it for the benefit of a man in the witness box. The caption reads: "Lawyer: Perhaps *this* will refresh your memory".

Pets and animals periodically feature in legal cases which arise from the oddest circumstances.

Custoady matters

If someone says he's intending to get high, you'd expect him perhaps to be about to climb a mountain or smoke a joint. David Theiss had another plan. He aimed to get high by licking the venom glands of a Colorado River Toad. Not everyone's idea of a good time – but then human pleasure covers a wide and varied canvass.

Mr Theiss wasn't hoping that the toad would turn into a princess once he put it to his mouth. He was aiming to go into an hallucinogenic fugue from the toad's glandular secretions. He was arrested by police in Kansas City in 2007 for possessing the toad, "with the intention of using it as a hallucinogen". Following the arrest, Theiss was given bail – but the toad was kept in custody.

English law on prohibited drugs and substances is complicated. There are over 250 substances covered in the Schedules to the Misuse of Drugs Act 1971. Most are synthetic, and many have technical titles such as 2-(2,5-Dimethoxy-4-methylphenyl)cyclopropylamine. Some drugs, though, are found in natural items like flora. Opium, for example, is the coagulated juice of the opium poppy. And some drugs are found in animals – bufotenine (a Class A drug) occurs as a secretion of the common toad and natterjack toad. The secretion can make people ill and kill some animals.

Under the Wildlife and Countryside Act 1981, it's an offence intentionally to kill, injure, take, or possess a toad, as it's a protected animal. However, the House of Lords has ruled that the offence of unlawful possession of a drug under the Misuse of Drugs Act 1971 isn't established just by proof of the possession of a natural material (which would include a toad) of which the drug is one of the unseparated ingredients. So, under English law, no one has ever been arrested for possession of a toad with intent to slurp it. After capture, Theiss's lawyer worked very hard to ensure his client avoided a custoadial punishment.

Monkeying around

Courts sometimes have to make difficult decisions about whether something is in a legal category. Is a sawn-off piano leg an offensive weapon?

But new ground was broken in January 2008 when the Supreme Court of Austria was asked to rule that Matthew Hiasl Pan is a person. That sounds easy enough for even an inexperienced lawyer. But the challenge was that Matthew is a chimpanzee.

An animal-rights group, VGT, had tried to have Matthew declared a person so a lawyer could be appointed as his guardian when the shelter where the chimp had lived for 25 years closed. Donors had raised money for the chimp, but, under Austrian law, only a person may benefit from a scheme such as VGT proposed. The campaign group, based in Vienna, sought to have Matthew declared a legal person, arguing that chimpanzees share 99.4 per cent of DNA with humans.

The court dismissed the case on the grounds that VGT wasn't authorised to make the appeal on Matthew's behalf, since he was neither a mentally handicapped person nor in any immediate danger.

The Supreme Court upheld an earlier ruling by a judge in the town of Wiener Neustadt, rejecting the petition.

Matthew is certainly amiable – it would be unfortunate if no legal mechanism could be found to enable him to be given a good place to live. The defeated group said it would take the case to the European Court of Human Rights. If it wins, though, the name of the court will have to be changed.

Bear Necessities

Who do you think said this: "I tried to distract him with lights and music because I heard bears are afraid of that"?

No marks if you said it was Eeyore or Tigger speaking of Winnie the Pooh, nor if you said it was Mr Brown about Paddington Bear. It was Zoran Kiseloski, appearing as the chief prosecution witness in 2008 in the case against a brown bear accused of stealing honey.

The court in Bitola, Macedonia, was told that the bear had been stealing the honey from the hives of Mr Kiseloski, a bee keeper. Mr Kiseloski had made his own attempts at crime prevention based on the bear fear of lights and music. This he didn't do half-heartedly. He purchased a generator and flood lit his bee hive area with powerful lamps. He then hooked up a big sound system to the power source and pumped music out at its highest volume. His choice of deterrent was "the songs of Ceca", which is evidently in the genre of "turbo-folk". In the world of sonic repulsions, admittedly, "turbo-folk" does seem like it would be sufficiently awful to keep back from a pot of honey even a wild bear with a low sugar count. But it was not to be so.

Illuminated in halogen, and soundtracked to the thrashing beats of turbo folk, the bear bounced back. According to the prosecution, it then dishonestly misappropriated a great quantity of honey. The court found the bear guilty. The lawyer for Mr Kiseloski asked for a compensation order to be made. As, however, the bear didn't have an owner, the court instructed the state to pay the compensation which was set at £1,700.

Historically, animals weren't put on trial in England but they were in other parts of Europe. Around 1510, for eating a barley crop in Autun, France, a pack of rats was prosecuted. Sadakat Kadri records, in *The Trial*, the ingenious arguments used by Bartholomew Chassenée, the rats' lawyer, to try to get them acquitted. He got one adjournment because the trumpets used to summon the rats to court didn't bring all of them there, and no one should be tried in the absence. The court agreed and asked for a better summonsing to court to take place through sermons.

Then, when the court tried to start the trial later (with some rats absent), Chassenée asked for a further adjournment. He noted the ancient principle that no defendant was required to risk life or limb in getting to court, and that his rat clients couldn't attend because their route to court was beset with the dangers of cats and dogs. He won another postponement. Eventually, though, the rats got banished – but only after many of them had been able to flee the court's jurisdiction because of their clever lawyer.

Coil the defence witness

In English law, there are over 9,000 different sorts of criminal offence. There are few, however, to which the argument: "I did it in order to stop my snakes from falling asleep", would be recognised as a lawful defence.

But there's a case which shows that a "stimulating my serpents" defence can be argued. Caroline Shepherd, the Chief Adjudicator of Parking Appeals recounted, in 2008, a case in which a woman appealed to the Traffic and Parking Appeals Service about a parking offence.

The driver was a belly dancer who had stopped in her car in a restricted parking zone in London. She had left her vehicle stationary with the engine running, and walked off with some props into the building where she was to perform. She was issued with a penalty but successfully appealed. She explained that her conduct was necessary because in her car she had snakes that she was about to use in her "exotic dance routine". She needed to leave the engine running, she explained, in order to keep her reptiles warm to stop them from falling asleep. If they fell asleep they would, the appeal was told, be difficult to rouse quickly enough for their impending stage performance with the dancer. Her appeal succeeded and the fine was cancelled.

Facing a criminal charge in Brisbane District Court, Australia, in 2006, Katsuhide Naito, a Japanese man, also gave an unusual excuse. He told the court that his otherwise criminal conduct should be seen sympathetically in the context that he only committed the offence in order "to acquire a champion Australian cattle dog".

Naito had contravened laws about bringing living matter into Australia. He'd aimed to swap his organic contraband for the cattle dog. He might have been treated leniently had he tried to smuggle a ladybird or four-leaf clover. But the authorities who searched his bag weren't impressed to find 39 live snakes, lizards and turtles.

The Brisbane judge declared that the wrongdoing was very serious. He ruled that the proper court order was one for euthanasia and stuffing. Mr Naito might well have fainted with shock at that point but the judge explained it was the reptiles that should be given the treatment and then donated to the Queensland Museum. Naito himself was spared and given a 3 month prison sentence.

Catastrophe

In law courts across the world no financial case had turned on the contents of a cat's litter tray until a 2009 decision at the administrative court in Frankfurt, Germany.

The story begins with Peter Neumann's cat and its expensive food tastes. The cat, Neumann argued, ate a €500 banknote. Holding some fragments of the note which he said had gone through the cat and been discovered in the litter tray, Neumann then went to the German Bundesbank to ask for a replacement note.

Under German law, a note can be replaced by the bank if there is positive proof that the note existed (usually at least half the note) and proof that the rest of the note had been destroyed. The bank official declined to replace the note in this case. It expressed suspicions about the small fragments of note it had been given, saying they appeared to be from different notes. If that were true it would mean that either the cat had been enjoying an unusually rich diet at Neumann's expense or that someone had been tearing off bits from different notes and the replacement request was a ruse.

Neumann has maintained his innocence and regretted that there is no realistic prospect of him getting more evidence. While not as challenging Hercules' task of cleaning out the Augean stables, the job before him is decidedly difficult "It's not that I don't want to go looking through pet excrement to get what's rightfully mine" he said "it just that the evidence really isn't around any longer".

Previously, the most curious cat to have challenged the courts was Blackie the Talking Cat who entertained people on the streets of Augusta, Georgia in America. In 1981, a legal dispute arose because the city wanted to tax the couple who owned Blackie as they earned money from citizens who paid to hear him speak. Were Blackie's owners engaged in an "occupation" and thus open to be taxed? The court ruled they should be taxed. It rejected their various arguments including one that the legislation was unconstitutional because it did not specifically mention talking cats.

Of particular interest in the nine-page law report is the very long first footnote in which the judge explains that on one occasion he met Blackie on the street laying across his owner's shoulder and, in exchange for money, the cat spoke to him. In the judgment, the judge states that he did not let this incident affect his reasoning in the case but he also noted that he enjoyed the encounter saying "I felt my dollar was well spent" and recording that the cat had said to him "I love you". On the disappointing tax judgment for his owners, Blackie made a discreet no comment.

Dogknapping

Science was used to solve an unusual burglary in May, 2004. Police in New Orleans, Louisiana, arrested Edwin Gallo for the theft of a pedigree poodle after its DNA was

used to identify it as one of five valuable puppies stolen
from a pet shop.

Dog theft in the UK has even extended to dognapping
for ransom but this crime is not a recent development. The
19th-century advocate Montague Williams QC once had
his beloved dog stolen by a London gang. He recounts in
his autobiography how he was approached by man who
said "Lost a dawg, sir, I believe? A collie dawg … I knows
a pal of mine as might be able to work the hanimal back".
Williams got back Rob, his collie, after a payment of £20
and nocturnal meeting with gang members at Bishopsgate
station. Two years later, Williams was instructed to
prosecute various "dog-stealers". The maximum sentence
for the crime was "only eighteen months hard labour"
as dogs were not classified as "chattels" in law, but, in a
cunning move to indict the thieves for the graver crime
of felony, Williams also prosecuted for theft of the dog-
collar worn by the stolen animals. Fate unfolded with
the elegance of a morality tale as the first defendant in
Williams' list was the man who had earlier stolen his dog.
Ruff justice.

A pigging dentist, a disguised dog and a dead fly

When other species get involved in our legal disputes,
the cases are often bizarre. Two fetched up in the courts
in May, 2008. These are the curious cases of the dog and
the fly.

"We are in deep shit now", wrote Newton Johnson in
a diary entry that was to mark the beginning of his fall.
He was a dentist in Llanelli, Wales, but not a happy one.
"This bloody job, who'd be a pigging dentist" he had
written one night in his log. He'd become alarmed when
the Health Service started to investigate his practice. He
had good reason to be worried. He was in the middle of a
scam in which, with his wife Judith, his practice manager,
he eventually swindled the public purse out of £37,555 for
work he had not carried out. They'd invented 100 patients
including Varlo Johnson – and Varlo was to prove part of
their downfall. The thing that made it difficult for Varlo to
pretend to be a patient was that although he has teeth, he

is a Hungarian Wirehaired Vizsla, and, therefore, has four legs. Varlo is the pet of Mr Johnson's sister.

Mr Johnson and his wife were convicted at Swansea Crown Court and jailed, but not before prosecuting counsel had used the nature of the case to inspire some extraordinary oratorical flourishes. Drilling deep into dental language, Mr Justin Gau, for the Crown, told the court, "The fillings they performed were the fillings of their own wallets", and that "They were saying to the public purse 'open wide' and performing a series of illegal extractions". Rinse that.

Before I mention the fly, let me mention a famous snail in the case of *Donoghue v Stevenson*. On 26 August 1928, Mrs May Donoghue sat in the Wellmeadow Café in Paisley and drank the defendant manufacturer's ginger beer, bought for her by her friend. The bottle contained the decomposed remains of a snail. Mrs Donoghue suffered from shock and severe gastro-enteritis. She sued the manufacturer of the ginger beer for negligence. Lord Atkin stated: "The rule that you are to love your neighbour becomes in law, you must not injure your neighbour". This became a legal duty to " … take reasonable care to avoid acts or omissions which you can reasonably foresee would be likely to injure your neighbour". Mrs Donoghue's case was settled for £200.

Now meet the fly. The dead insect was at the bottom of a drinking water bottle, in a kitchen in Windsor, Ontario, when it was seen by Mr Martin Mustapha and his wife. He became obsessed with the event and its implications for the health of his family. He then developed a major depressive disorder, phobia and anxiety that affected his sleep, sex life, business, and willingness to take showers. He sued Culligan of Canada, the supplier of the bottle of water, for $341,000 for psychiatric injury. The trial judge awarded him damages but the Canadian Supreme Court has since rejected his claim.

Chief Justice Beverley McLachlin states, in the unanimous ruling, that the injuries were not "reasonably foreseeable" by ordinary standards. She said Mr Mustapha failed to show that it was foreseeable that "a person of ordinary fortitude" would suffer serious injury from seeing the fly in the bottle of water.

Mr Mustapha said the case cost him $500,000, as the result of therapy and legal fees. The case has buzzed in the heads of all the lawyers, doctors, and company directors for 6 years, and has now had the attention of 12 senior Canadian judges. The total cost is over $1m and has taken over 50,000 person-at-work hours if you include all the court officials and administrative staff. Do not underestimate the impact a fly can make on the world.

Sleeping with the fishes

In September 2008 in Texas, Gene Hathorn added another option to the principle of 'ashes to ashes and dust to dust': convicted murderer to goldfish food.

Hathorn was on death-row, and was on his third and final appeal at the Court of Criminal Appeals. He said, however, that if that appeal failed then his body should be used by the artist Marco Evaristti as "installation art" in a project on capital punishment. Hathorn specified that the artist should deep-freeze his executed corpse and then turn it into fish food which visitors at an exhibition could then feed to goldfish.

In 1985, in Trinity County in Texas, Hawthorn was convicted of killing his father. Mr Evaristti, a Chilean artist living in Denmark, visited him for the first time in 2008 when the fish food plan was devised.

Evaristti presented his felon-into-food idea as part of a serious moral indictment of the system of capital punishment (as opposed to a daft and artless stunt). He said that more important than the story of Hathorn is the need to highlight America's "vulgar and primitive" system of capital punishment.

The artist's values, though, and his claimed aversion to vulgarity will be seen by some people in a wider context. In Copenhagen in 2000, he installed something at an exhibition that was removed by police under Danish law. Evaristti's exhibit was a row of transparent electric food blenders which had been plugged into sockets ready for action. Evaristti had filled each of them with water and live goldfish, and visitors were invited to switch on the blenders to produce fish soup.

Evaristti's 'feeding the felon to the fishes' idea was eventually scuppered in 2009 when Hathorn made a plea deal (pleading guilty to murdering his stepmother and half-brother when he killed his father) under which he took three life sentences to come off death row.

Although historically under English law no convict's body was ever, as in the Hathorn plan, turned into fish food, some executed felons did, in *The Godfather* phrase, end up "sleeping with the fishes". It was the early medieval practice of various coastal towns such as Portsmouth and Sandwich Bay to execute convicts who been sentenced to death by tying them to a stake on the shore at low tide and leaving them there to drown.

Convicts in London managed to escape execution by consenting to their bodies being used for medical experiments. When John Benham was under sentence of death in the 18th century, he gained a pardon from George III in exchange for agreeing to have a limb amputated. Surgeons wanted to test how good a newly-invented styptic was at stemming severe blood loss. The styptic must have been reasonably good because the records show that following the amputation Benham was later released from Newgate gaol. It is always good to see law at the cutting edge of medical science.

Beaking his mind

"Oh my God, that's him!" Angela Colicheski exclaimed as the young subject of her custody battle with Sarita Lytell was brought into court in 2009. Both women knew that only one of them would be leaving the court in Florida with the youngster each had, at different times, nurtured and doted on. The judge looked on gravely as he realised that in deciding which desperate woman should win custody, he would have to exercise the wisdom of Solomon.

This custody clash was similar to many other previous cases except for the fact that the dispute between two devoted carers was over a 13-year-old African Grey parrot.

For 10 years, Colicheski had loved and cared for the parrot she called Tequila. Then, 3 years ago, he flew away over her garden fence. Colicheski ran frantically all over the district but could not find him. She was distraught and heart-broken. Three long years passed. Then, one day, Colicheski was sitting in a local Dunkin Donuts chatting to Lytell, whom she'd just met, when they started to talk about parrots. Lytell said she had one called Lucky that she had found 3 years earlier. It quickly became clear that he was the one Colicheski had lost but Lytell refused to hand him over, having formed a bonded relationship with the bird.

Presiding in Palm Beach county court, the judge heard a lawyer for Lytell argue that, as she had cared for the bird for 3 years, it had become hers. Colicheski's lawyer, however, argued that the parrot was a chattel (a piece of legal property) and must be returned. The judge agreed, saying that the parrot was treated, under state law, as personal property. "If the plaintiff had lost her automobile somehow along the way", he asked rhetorically, "would it be any less her property when she found it?". He ruled that Tequila was the property of Colicheski as she was his original owner and carer for 10 years.

Tequila didn't give sworn testimony but he did give squawk testimony. As soon as he was brought into court and saw his previous owner he emitted what witnesses said was a loud call of recognition.

This is not the first such dispute in the law courts of the world. In 2006 in Argentina, in litigation between Jorge Machado and Rio Vega, the court ruled that a parrot called Pepo, which each man claimed was his, should be imprisoned until it uttered the name of its owner. Five days later, it squawked "Jorge" and sang the anthem of his favourite football team – San Lorenzo. The evidence of another parrot caused problems in Leeds in 2006. Chris Taylor discovered his partner Suzy was having an affair when his parrot, kept saying, in a perfect mimic of her voice, "I love you Gary".

Chapter 7

ON THE ROAD

In 2009, Gary Sanders was driving his car when he was pulled over by Liverpool police and questioned for laughing in his car while driving. Officers told him "laughing while driving can be an offence". With that in mind, it might be a good precaution for passengers in general to avoid recounting to their drivers the facts of some of the cases in this chapter. There are now over 600,000,000 vehicles on the roads across the world so we have a considerable base of activity from which bizarre incidents can arise.

Wheely good times

While laws imposing speed limits are standard in all countries, the ways they are broken are sometimes distinctive.

Guenther Eichmann, 54, was stopped by police in the high street in Geseke, Germany, in 2007 for driving at 40mph, twice the speed limit.

His case resulted in a £300 fine and the confiscation of his vehicle. But if you looked at the prosecution papers expecting to see that the vehicle he was driving was a BMW or a Mercedes, you'd be surprised. What the police had to race to catch was a supercharged electric wheelchair. Mr Eichmann, a former engineer, had modified the wheelchair himself.

Over 1.5 million speeding tickets are issued in England and Wales each year. The offence has a long history. The first person in Britain to be fined for speeding was the pioneer of the petrol-engine car, Walter Arnold. On 27

January 1896, when there were only 20 cars in Britain, Mr Arnold was driving through Paddock Wood in Kent. He was going 8mph – four times over the 2mph limit imposed for built-up areas by the Locomotive Act 1865. A policeman eating his lunch in a nearby cottage abandoned his meal, donned his helmet, and chased the car for some distance on a bicycle. The long arm of the law was propelled by powerful legs. The officer eventually apprehended Mr Arnold who was later fined one shilling.

Some cases of speeding in Britain have been odd in respect of both the vehicle and the venue. In May 2007, people were having a relaxing game of golf at the Royal Dornoch golf course in Scotland when racing across the 15th fairway towards them came what was reported as "a madman on a horse". There was much alarm and distress. Even the horse was anxious. An accident was narrowly avoided, and Maurice Murphy, 27, was convicted of culpably and recklessly "riding a horse furiously". He was put on probation for 2 years, so it's 100/1 odds against that he'll be racing at a golf course any time soon.

Tyred and emotional

In civil law, a defendant can raise alternative and even contradictory defences.

Once, a leading barrister's son, accused by his headmaster of breaking a school window, replied: (1) the schoolroom has no window; (2) the window was not broken; (3) if it is broken I did not do it; and (4) it was an accident.

Pleading diverse excuses to mitigate a punishment, however, is not a good idea. In 2009, a man in Boulder, Colorado, confessed to vandalising 46 cars. Alexander Kabelis was caught after acting suspiciously, crouched behind a police vehicle parked near a police centre. An officer who went to investigate found the tyre slashed and later apprehended Kabelis, who was carrying a steak knife in his pocket. He admitted puncturing the tyres of nine police vehicles and 37 other cars in the same area, causing $12,000 worth of damage.

Why had Kabelis done such a thing? He told police that he had committed the car crimes because of a troubled relationship with his mother, the irritation that police cars whizzing past had always caused him, the fact that he had to wear a dental brace as a child, the loss of his driving licence, the radiation emitted from a nearby plant, and, simply, irresistible temptation.

His confession was the defence equivalent of Groucho Marx's famous assertion: "These are my principles, and if you don't like them [thumps desk with hand] ... I have others".

Unfortunately for Kabelis, none of the diverse reasons he gave for his crime was ever likely to mitigate his sentence.

Don't look back

There is a legal principle that law looks forward not back – *lex prospicit non respicit*. A new rule should not be applied to a time before it was made, otherwise people could be later condemned for doing something that was lawful when they did it. In 2007, Nasser Khan parked his car in Salford, England in a gap between yellow lines. Then someone, in effect, wrote a new law with thermoplastic paint. While Khan was away, a workman painted yellow lines under his car, then a traffic warden issued a ticket for the unlawfully parked vehicle. Sir William Blackstone noted in 1765 that it would be "cruel and unjust" if "an action, innocent when it was done, should be afterward converted to guilt". But no one had apparently told that to the traffic warden.

An important legal footnote

Many general points of law have been decided in cases involving police constables and cars. In *Fagan v Metropolitan Police Commissioner* (1968) the court resolved that although an omission to act cannot amount to an assault, that crime will be committed if someone accidentally commits a battery which he then refuses to discontinue. Mr Vincent Fagan drove his car on to the foot of PC David Morris in Fortunegate Road, London. That was probably an accident but, the report states, when the PC said "Get off, you are on my foot", Mr Fagan replied, "Fuck you, you can wait". Twenty five seconds later, by which time the PC's left big toe had been bruised, Mr Fagan relented with the words "Okay, man, okay". His conviction was upheld using what has become known as the doctrine of the continuing act.

A defence not in the law syllabus

Judge Robert Holzberg said in a case in Connecticut in 2004: "No one ever told me in law school that we'd be having these kinds of conversation in open court". Heather Specyalski was charged with the homicide of Neil Esposito. He was thrown from a car that prosecutors said was being driven by Specyalski when it spun out of control and crashed. The defendant was judicially permitted to argue that she could not have been driving because she was in the passenger seat performing oral sex on Esposito, whom she alleged was at the wheel. Esposito was found with his trousers down but prosecutors argue this could have been because he was "mooning" or urinating out of the car window while in the passenger seat. Specyalski was eventually acquitted. British cases have sometimes hinged on intricate sexual matters. In an 1836 case it was necessary to judge whether a couple could have committed adultery on a stile in a public footpath in Yorkshire, and in a 1945 case, an adultery allegation turned on whether couple with a "long history of passionate intimacy" could have copulated "in a semi-recumbent position" on the front seat of a lorry.

Within inches of justice

There is a legal principle known as *de minimis non curat lex* – the law takes no account of trifling matters. It means, for example, that there should not be a prosecution for theft of a penny or litigation over a freight train full of fruit that if it is one apple light.

That motto, however, might not have been part of the training of the wheel-clamper who, in May 2008, secured the car of Ian Taylor of Tredworth in Gloucestershire.

The car, a 1994 Ford Fiesta, had a necessary certificate for vehicles kept off the road but it wasn't taxed to be on the road. At the key moment, when the vehicle was clamped, although almost the entire vehicle was off the road and on Mr Taylor's front drive, 2 inches were protruding from his land.

Having purchased the broken car for £50 to repair as a gift for his stepson, Mr Taylor was very upset to be told by the clampers, acting for the Driver and Vehicle Licensing Agency (DVLA), that the cost for unclamping the vehicle was £280.

Mr Taylor then took a large revving metal cutter – and the law – into his own hands. Enraged, he cut the car in half. With a thought as incisive as his handiwork, Mr Taylor then told the DVLA to take the back half of the car, as it was that which was fractionally overhanging the road. Moments later, five police cars and ten officers were on the scene. In legal terms, things had escalated from *de minimis* to *de maximis*. But common sense eventually prevailed and no prosecutions followed.

Applications of the principle of *de minimis* have varied. Sometimes what seem like minimal matters do get into court. In 1983, a couple from Kent, England, removed a defective fence post on their land, and after they'd repaired it replaced it 2 inches nearer their neighbour's land. But the 2-inch dispute turned into a 2-year stretch of litigation, and the judgment was so convoluted it took 2 hours to read out in court.

In another similar case, it was not the position of the fence post that was in issue but the width of string around it. The string was alleged to be a trespass on the adjoining land. The case knotted the lawyers for a while but the *de minimis* rule was applied and the incident was not judged as a trespass.

In 1992, in Alberta, Canada, Judge CL Daniel acquitted Marion Harrison of assault when it became apparent that the charge related to an incident in which she'd allegedly hit her ex-husband with a shopping bag filled with clothes. In 2007, in Dubai, however, a British citizen, Keith Brown, was sentenced to 4 years' imprisonment for possession of 0.003 grams of cannabis, about the weight of a grain of sand.

One person irate that the rule didn't apply in his case is Dietmar Hehenberger. In 2006, following a court order, Mr Hehenberger, an Austrian hotelier, sawed off part of his hotel roof because it was hanging into the Czech Republic. The overhang was 12 inches – a decided inconvenience if your bed was being reduced by that much but less of an incursion into the Czech Republic as that extends over 30,450 square miles.

Fitness to drive

The question of who is fit to drive has generated some bizarre cases. In 2008, the Italian government was ordered by a Sicilian court to pay €100,000 compensation to a man who had been issued with a disabled driving licence on the basis that he is gay.

Danilo Giuffrida, 27, had volunteered information on his sexual orientation to the military authorities during a physical examination after being called up in 2000 for Italy's then mandatory year of military service. He was categorised as having a "disturbance of sexual identity" and the military authorities then informed the transport ministry that he was "not in possession of the necessary psycho-physical requirements". As a result, his driving licence was immediately revoked.

Mr Giuffrida agreed to retake his driving test, and passed it for a second time. But the driving authority classified his sexual orientation as a mental illness and issued him with a licence for one year, instead of the usual 10, on the grounds that he was gay. The disabled licence must be renewed every year instead of the standard period of every 10 years.

The judge who presided over the case in Catania, Sicily, said the conduct of the government ministries showed unwarranted discrimination against the claimant and "contempt for his constitutional rights". In addition to the compensation, the ministries were ordered to pay €10,000 to meet Mr Giuffrida's legal costs during his protracted litigation through the courts.

The rather bizarre sexual analysis of the Italian military and driving authorities has its origins in early religious ideas. In some societies that were keen to promote a fast and stable increase in numbers, anything that didn't assist was condemned as sinful. This meant lumping together the rather odd assortment of bestiality, masturbation, withdrawal (*coitus interruptus*), and homosexuality. To practise any of these was a major dissent. The word "bugger" was originally a word meaning a heretic.

Historically, English law has labelled all sorts of unconventional social categories as mentally defective, including, at one time, unmarried mothers. But in applying the law, the road traffic authorities today haven't got time for any daft theories about drivers' sexual orientation as there are more pressing matters of who's fit to drive. Omed Aziz was stopped by traffic police in April 2006, in the West Midlands, for dangerous driving and was prosecuted at Warley Magistrates' Court. A police officer described how, after pulling Aziz over for driving on the wrong side of the road, he asked him to remove his sunglasses. In court, the prosecuting lawyer asked constable Glyn Austin if he had noticed anything in particular when Aziz removed his shades. PC Austin replied: "I did – he didn't have any eyes".

"I attempted to speak to the driver, who appeared to be fumbling around with the controls", the officer said. "At that point the passenger leaned across and stated, 'He's blind'".

Aziz, who lost both his eyes in a bomb blast, was, he said, receiving instructions on how to drive from his passenger. That, though, did not exactly get him off the hook for several reasons – including the fact that his passenger had himself been banned from driving. Justice is blind, but drivers shouldn't be.

Road runner

A woman from Dover, New Hampshire, who cross-examined police in court with 96 questions about a speeding ticket, lost her appeal against conviction at the state Supreme Court in 2008.

In October 2008, a district court found Christina Downs, 24, guilty of speeding. She had been recorded driving at 44mph in a 25mph zone. In court, Ms Downs represented herself. She swung into the trial process with gusto, delivering a torrent of questions and objections, finally moving for dismissal of the case.

Ms Downs was evidently something of a fiery character. During the trial, police officer Timothy Cashman testified that, after he had issued her with the speeding ticket, she had started her car and immediately raced off so rapidly he had to pursue her and pull her over again for speeding.

In her cross-examination of Cashman, Downs questioned his experience, his training, his work schedule, the radar technology used to determine her speed, weather conditions, traffic flow, his theoretical knowledge of law and the science of speed. When, following this, Justice Sawako Gardner herself asked some points of officer Cashman, Downs sprung up and objected to the judge "questioning the witness". Downs was eventually found guilty and ordered to pay a $100 penalty.

She then appealed to the state's highest court, arguing that local police failed to provide her with engineering studies used to decide the speed limit on Elwyn Road, where she was ticketed.

The Supreme Court ruled that the burden of proof fell on Downs to get the report from a proper source (not the police) and to show why it was relevant. The court concluded Downs had not overcome the presumption that the speed limit was valid and so ruled that her conviction was lawful.

Ever since Walter Arnold became the first person to be convicted of speeding (8mph in Kent, England, in 1896), people's opposition to speeding fines has produced some curious cases. In 2006, at Manchester Crown Court, Craig Moore was sentenced to 4 months' imprisonment for blowing up a roadside speed camera. Having been photographed speeding, he'd driven back to the camera with industrial explosive to destroy the evidence in the yellow camera box. He'd been caught because the explosion jolted the camera to take another photograph which included his vehicle by the crime scene. A case, decidedly, of someone blowing his own cover.

Earlier in 2008, Vikki Fielden appealed at Bradford Crown Court against a speeding conviction arguing that the camera which clocked her at 36mph in a 30mph zone was inaccurate as it was on a bend in the road. Hours of physics played out in argument in court, based on the preparation of her husband (a university science researcher), didn't favour her, and her conviction was upheld.

While driving at 12mph on Lexington Avenue, Manhattan, on 20 May, 1899, Jacob German became the first person in America to be arrested for speeding. He was working as a taxicab driver for the Electric Vehicle Company when he was pulled over by bicycle patrolman Schueller. History doesn't record whether the New York taxi driver narrowed his eyes at the officer and asked "Are you talking to me?".

Fateful fruit

According to one theory, a woman who bit an apple caused the downfall of human kind. In this case, trouble arose from something even less than a bite of an apple. Sarah McCaffery, a nursery nurse from Northumberland, was convicted of a motoring offence, fined £60 and ordered to pay £100 costs in 2005, after she drove round a bend, in second gear, with an apple in her hand. During ten court hearings, prosecutors used photographic evidence from a spotter plane. The exercising of prosecutorial discretion can be contentious. In 1995, for example, Gary Lewis, an impoverished father, was prosecuted at a cost of £750 after he stole six lumps of coal to keep his newborn baby warm. In 2000, Kevin Storey was fined £20 after he put into his mouth, while driving on the M3, a piece of Kit Kat that his wife, a passenger, had unwrapped for him. The Hampshire assistant chief constable eventually cut Lewis some slack and cancelled the fine but we do not know if the accompanying note said: "Have a break".

Speedy reply

Long before Jeremy Bentham invented the noun
"cross-examination" in 1827, the art was being refined.
One instance, though, of a failure to respect the
principle of avoiding real inquiries is recounted by Sir
Oliver Popplewell. As a young barrister he was cross-
examining a witness who had testified that his client,
accused of careless driving, had been speeding. The
witness was repeatedly pressed to estimate the speed but
declined. Having satisfactorily established the witness's
incompetence in car-speed estimation, Mr Popplewell did
not sit down but asked one final fatal question: "Why are
you telling the court you cannot estimate the speed of my
client's car?". The response was quick and clear: "Because
I have never seen a car go as fast as that in all my life".

Public place

AS gourmets love fine delicacies, so lawyers love nice
definitions. One phrase often to have been devotedly cut,
trimmed, boiled down and garnished by the courts is
"public place". In 2004, a pub car park was ruled to be a
"public place", during licensing hours, for the purposes of
drink driving law. Police officers discovered David Lewis
driving his vehicle in the car park of the Black Bull pub in
Ruislip, Middlesex. He was over the legal alcohol limit.
The High Court ruled that it could be assumed, without
proof, that a pub car park open to the public was a "public
place". In 1947, upholding the drink-driving conviction
of a Mr Cartlidge, who had been caught in grounds
adjoining the Fox and Hounds near Otley, Yorkshire, the
High Court observed that a public place was "a place to
which the public have access".

In other areas of law, however, the phrase has been
differently interpreted. Another High Court case, in
1971, concerned a group of nine thugs accused of using
threatening behaviour on the platform of West Kirby
station in The Wirral. The court ruled that a station
platform was not, as required by the Public Order Act
1936, a "public place" because it was an integral part
of a building – the station – and incidents in buildings

(apart from public meetings) were beyond the scope of the legislation. A definitional delicacy to be savoured.

A mission from God

In the film *The Blues Brothers*, a determined duo try to justify their repeated errant behaviour by explaining "we're on a mission from God". But arguing in court that a divine duty should excuse criminal conduct will rarely succeed.

Necessity can sometimes be a defence to a crime but is a religious mission a necessity? In a challenge to the Italian legal system in 2009, three nuns caught driving at 112 mph explained to the police they were racing to the Pope, as he was injured.

Police had chased a Ford Fiesta as it shot along a road near Turin at almost double the speed limit. When they caught the car, Sister Tavoletta, 56, explained that she and her fellow nuns, aged 65 and 78, had just learnt that Pope Benedict XVI had slipped in his bathroom and fractured his wrist. They were proceeding with God's speed, if not the law's, to the pontiff's holiday chalet at Les Combes to see if they could offer help or prayers. The law, though, would not absolve their offence. Sister Tavoletta was fined €375 and her driving licence was revoked for a month. Her lawyer, Anna Orecchioni, said she will appeal using the defence of necessity.

In driving cases, the defence of necessity is very rarely successful although it has been pleaded in some decidedly odd cases. In 2004, in Australia, Lee Collinson, 24, was prosecuted in Darwin on a charge of driving without a licence. When caught on the road by police, he had explained that he was on an urgent mission of necessity to deliver condoms to his cousin. Presenting his evidence in a direct style of Australian English, he explained: "My cousin was about to [have sex with] this girl and he needed his bag because it had his condoms in it".

The magistrate acknowledged the urgency of Collinson's undertaking for his friend in need, commending it as good "mateship". The Bench then tried to demonstrate its magisterial human understanding of the situation by quoting a Spike Milligan remark about "a woman at boiling point". But the application of driving law isn't a heat-sensitive system. Collinson was convicted and fined $100.

Chapter 8

Lawyers do important jobs but they don't always enjoy a positive portrayal. "If a lawyer's ego was hit by lightening" the writer Kathy Lette once noted, "the lightening would be hospitalised". Most of the jokes about lawyers revolve around a perception that some members of the profession can be very concerned about their remuneration. Hence, the story of the man who goes to seek help from his local lawyer:

Client:	What is your most basic fee?
Lawyer:	£100 to answer three questions.
Client:	Whoa! That's pretty expensive isn't it?
Lawyer:	Yes, now what is your third question?

This type of joke has a long history. In ancient Greece, Diogenes once went looking for an honest lawyer. "How is it going?" asked someone who passed him on the road. "Not bad" replied Diogenes "I still have my lantern".

Most lawyers, though, are highly-qualified and dedicated professionals. Many aspects of their work predispose them to end up in some unusual social dramas. They are, for example, a naturally argumentative collection of people, they are occupationally preoccupied with using rules all the time in relation to virtually everything, and they are mostly involved with clients who have problems that cannot be solved in any ordinary social way. That's a mixture likely to produce some interesting characters. So, it is not surprising that we find lawyers in some extraordinary situations.

The long arm of the law

In many countries, advocates are allowed to take a pillow-talk briefing and represent their spouses in court.

The trouble is that if advocates lose such spousal cases, their despair, plus their client's impending personal criticism, can trigger certain unprofessional moments.

Having lost a criminal case in which she defended her husband in February 2008, Kathy Brewer Rentas, an American media litigation lawyer, was charged with assault for allegedly shaking the prosecutor's hand so vigorously that she injured the woman's shoulder.

Mrs Rentas approached Jennifer Keene, the prosecutor, for a handshake and then, allegedly, made the long arm of the law even longer by virtually pulling it from its socket.

Anthony Rentas was on federal probation for distributing cocaine in New York. He had admitted violating the terms of his probation, and Mrs Rentas had gone to court in Fort Lauderdale, Florida to represent him.

Having heard the case, District Judge William Zloch ordered that Mr Rentas be put under house arrest for 90 days and complete his probation. Court officials said Mrs Rentas then insisted on shaking hands with Assistant US Attorney Jennifer Keene.

According to an arrest report, Ms Keene didn't shake Brewer's hand at first, "but Brewer insisted that she do so and continued to follow Keene". The report said Brewer "forcefully grabbed on to Keene's right hand and squeezed it, pulling Keene toward her", and knocking her off balance. With Keene in hand, "Brewer made an upward, then a quick downward motion and pulled Keene toward the ground". One witness said the arm was almost ripped from its shoulder socket. Lawyers are usually good at being disarming but not quite like that.

Mrs Rentas was charged with assaulting a federal officer. She spent the night detained in solitary confinement. She was later released on a $100,000 bond and ordered to undergo a psychological evaluation to see if she needed counselling or anger management training. The psychologist who did the evaluation would, of course, have had to be careful about how he greeted this particular lawyer.

There is a convention among the barristers of England and Wales not to shake hands with each other. The origin of this custom isn't definitively recorded. One explanation, though, is that shaking hands was a very old way of people demonstrating, when they met, that they weren't holding a weapon, and that there was no need for such assurances between friends, especially learned friends.

Yours, in gratitude

In return for their hard-won qualifications, and highly useful professional expertise, lawyers often get quite rich. But sometimes they are paid disproportionately well, even in law. A lawyer who was paid almost half a million euros for writing one letter is a case in point. In 2004, a German lawyer, Dr Juergen Graefe, acted for an elderly pensioner client from St Augustin, near Bonn, who was sent a tax demand for €287m.

The client's income was actually only €17,000. The lawyer wrote one standard letter to the authorities for the demand to be rectified. Under German law, though, he is entitled to calculate his fee based on the amount of the reduction that he obtained for his client. A court confirmed his fee for the single letter at €440,234 (£308,000). It was paid by the state. There is no evidence, however, that Dr Graefe then pushed his luck by writing a thank-you letter.

When two trial tribes go to war

There is a scene in the Monty Python film *Life of Brian* in which Brian tries to join an organisation.

Brian:	Are you the Judean People's Front?
Reg:	Fuck off!
Brian:	What?
Reg:	Judean People's Front [scoffs]. We're the *People's Front of Judea*! Judean People's Front [scoffs]

In January, 2008, a rancorous legal dispute over organisational names broke out in America. It carried all the signs of being more animated than most. A citizen against citizen legal action is always vexed. Things get more fraught when one lawyer sues another lawyer. But the impending case in America was between two organisations of trial lawyers. Battles don't get more epic or gruesome.

In 2006, America's largest and most powerful organisation of trial lawyers changed its name from the *Association of Trial Lawyers of America* (ATLA) to the *American Association for Justice* (AAJ). It changed because it took the view that 'trial lawyers' was a phrase unlikely to excite good feelings whereas the word 'justice' hits the spot.

Not long afterwards, a group of lawyers formed a new organisation to compete with the AAJ, and adopted the gist of the abandoned name, adding 'The' to its title. So, the new organisation is called *The American Trial Lawyers Association*, abbreviated to TheATLA. The words are in a new order but it still gives you ATLA.

A membership recruitment letter from TheATLA said that it is an "elite organisation" whose members "exemplify superior qualifications, trial results, leadership, influence, reputation, stature, and profile in the trial attorney community". So they know their way around a courtroom, and you'd want to think twice before suing them.

The AAJ, however, did think twice and then issued proceedings in Minneapolis in order to force TheATLA to drop the name, arguing that the existence of the old name was confusing AAJ members and infringing a trademark. The claim also demanded that AAJ is awarded any money that TheATLA collects in membership dues, and, yes, treble damages and attorneys' fees.

The trial lawyers who argue the case for AAJ will no doubt be very good. A trial lawyer whose client is composed of 56,000 trial lawyers can expect some professional feedback.

TheATLA's principal founding member, J Keith Givens, maintained that AAJ liberated the ownership of its former name when it abandoned it in favour of the AAJ. How this battle will end is unclear as American legislation specifies that even if an organisation stops using a title for 3 years, such non-use raises only a "rebuttable presumption" that the trademark has been abandoned. That means that the alleged abandoner is free to show that it didn't in fact give up the title.

Under English law, the economic tort of 'passing off' is intended to protect businesses with established reputations from having trade diverted from them by other businesses that have adopted misleadingly similar names. The tort was developed to cater to the needs of commercial concerns but has been applied to other organisations. In one case, *British Diabetic Association v Diabetic Society Ltd and others* (1995), the British Diabetic Association won an injunction to stop a breakaway group from calling itself the Diabetic Society.

If they cannot settle on their own names, perhaps the American lawyers' organisations ought to commission some market research. Of course, it wouldn't be a job suitable for the faint-hearted. Imagine some of the replies you'd get, stopping people all day in the shopping mall and asking, "What would you call a collection of lawyers?".

Humble pie dinner

Two lawyers who descended into acrimonious mutual insults while taking the sworn statement of a witness in 2009 were judged by a federal court in Pennsylvania. Quoting *The Taming of the Shrew* at them – "Do as adversaries do in law, Strive mightily but eat and drink as friends" – the court ordered them to dine together to improve their relationship.

The case concerned a school janitor who sued a local education authority for alleged discrimination. The lawyers for both sides met to take depositions from school authority employees. When the defendant's counsel, James Ellison, objected to a question put to his client, the claimant's counsel, Lewis Hannah, responded "Shut up you are such an asshole". Ellison's then reassured his client: "[Mr Hannah]'s off his meds today. Pay no attention to that".

The meeting later broke up in bitterness and the lawyers became locked in a legal battle against each other, parallel to the case they were fighting for their clients. In considering counsels' conduct, Judge Gene Pratter noted that Hannah's behaviour was awful. He had four times referred to defence counsel as what the judge termed "a certain unattractive end-piece of anatomy". Hannah insisted he'd treated the opposition witness, Dr Walker, with respect but he admitted to repeatedly referring to her as "Ms Walker" in order "to get an edge" and to make her feel uneasy.

Judge Pratter ruled that the incivilities in this case were worse than those in a 1992 precedent in which counsel uttered one profanity ("cut the bullshit") but less bad than a 2008 case in which the word "fuck" and its grammatical variants had strafed through the deposition 73 times. Quoting a Supreme Court Justice, Pratter reminded the lawyers that civility was "not some bumper sticker slogan 'Have you hugged your adversary today'" but it was the mark of an accomplished professional.

The judge ruled that this wasn't an appropriate case in which to make Hannah pay the fees and costs of Ellison for the aborted deposition hearing; Ellison, after all, was not an innocent bystander in these events. The lawyers would, though, need to get on better so they were ordered to "join each other for an informal meal" to facilitate the "repair of their professional relationship". Hannah was also ordered to take a course in "civility and professionalism".

The permissible level of rudeness to a lawyer in England was addressed in a case in 1639. Mr Justice Barckley observed that it was unacceptable to say of a lawyer that "he hath no more law than a monkey" but it was okay to say "he had as much law as a monkey". The second statement is merely an incomplete truth – lawyers *do* know as much law as monkeys plus a lot more. What lawyers then called Barckley and his logic, however, involved words never used in even the roughest troop of monkeys.

Age is not a cage

"This lawyer is useless", thought Wang Jianbang, "I'm sure I could do better than that".

Since 2006, he'd been involved in an exasperating 2-year litigation struggle, and his lawyer had just screwed things up by confusing a civil case with an administrative one. Mr Wang, of Zhengzhou city, China, then resolved to study law himself in order to become a lawyer, so he applied to the Zhengzhou Justice School. He was duly admitted in 2008 although given a remission of his fees on account of his age. It wasn't, though, that he was still in high school, it was because he was 88.

In recent times, others too have challenged conventional thinking about age and the law. While Mr Wang is sagely poring over his law books in China, Joao Victor Portellinha, from Goias state Brazil, is also preparing to reject age prejudice in the law. In 2008 he passed his entrance examination to law school. "My dream is to be a federal judge", he said, "So I decided to take the test to see how I would do ... it was easy. I studied a week before the test". Brazilian lawyers, though, are very uneasy about this success. They would be happy if Mr Portellinha were 88. In fact, he was only 8 years old.

Some English lawyers have achieved things at extraordinary ages. In 1760, Jeremy Bentham, the philosopher-jurist, went up to Oxford aged 12, and the late law lord, Lord Bridge of Harwich, gained his degree in mathematics from The Open University in 2003 when aged 87.

But law courts haven't always been proficient at quickly telling people's ages. In *Lord v Thornton*, a case in Yorkshire in 1616, an advocate argued heroically throughout the case that his client, the defendant, was an infant. There was some disagreement about this in court. When, ultimately, a church records book was consulted to resolve the matter, it turned out that the defendant was not an infant. He was 63. Never think that some cases are too difficult for a lawyer to argue.

Permitting history

Lawyers at a council which is facing the prospect of suing itself are in for some late masochistic nights.

Carmarthenshire Council in Wales rejected planning permission for a playing field at a local school in 2009. The trouble was that the planning permission was being sought retrospectively because the playing field had, in fact, already been built without permission. The new field stands 1.4 metres above the surrounding ground and is built on the rubble of a demolished school building. There were 19 formal objectors – the field now overlooks their houses – but their opinions were never taken into account as the law requires.

In this type of situation the council should take legal action against whoever built something unlawfully. But as the council owns the school and built the field, and then applied for 'permission' afterwards, the council was obliged to take legal proceedings against itself. In-house council lawyers fell to working in a house divided. They should, though, buy some champagne for the end of the dispute because whichever way the case goes, some of the council lawyers will win.

Suing yourself isn't unprecedented. In 2005, the head of the Lebanese General Security Directorate issued proceedings against himself in order to try to clear himself of negligence in relation to the murder of a former Prime Minister. Judges have even convicted themselves. William Ettrick, presiding in Sunderland in England, in the early 1800s once fined a farmer for taking a cart to market without his name on it. When the farmer protested that the judge's own dung cart was outside the court without a name on it, the judge made a monosyllabic response (perhaps a *sotto voce* reference to the contents of his cart) and then imposed the same fine on himself.

Getting planning permission for something already built is among awkward cases where an impending decision has to look consistent with a past event. In a 19th-century case from a remote town in the American west, a jury was out for 33 hours in a murder trial before returning a verdict of "not guilty". The defendant, though, wasn't in court to hear the verdict. The judge was unhappy and sent the jurors away again to reconsider their verdict. He urged them to come to a decision "more consistent with the facts". The jury retired again and after a while came back with a "guilty" verdict. This time the judge said he was satisfied with the decision and then noted for the record that the defendant had already been hanged.

Drama in court

This is the story of a courtroom drama about a courtroom drama. In March 2008, Ravi Batra, a New York attorney, brought a $15 million legal action against the makers of the America television programme *Law and Order*. He claimed that a lawyer portrayed in the drama, "Ravi Patel", is by name and appearance clearly based on him but casts him as a corrupt lawyer bribing a judge.

There are only 20 lawyers in America with the first name Ravi. In real life, Mr Ravi Batra was named in a corruption scandal but not charged. He says the TV drama implied he was guilty.

The essence of most defamation cases is that the claimant argues that something portrayed as fact is really just a fiction. In this case, however, the claimant argued that something in fiction is being publicised as if it were a fact.

One precedent on a similar point was from 1983 in New York: *Springer v Viking Press*. An appeal court dismissed the case of a woman who sued a publisher when a chapter of a book contained a character with her name, who lived in her street, but who was described as a "whore" who engaged in "abnormal sexual practices". Lisa Springer, a Columbia University tutor, failed in her $20 million law suit based on the book *State of Grace* which was written by her former lover, Robert Tine.

The court ruled that to show defamation, the description of the fictional character must be so close to the real person that a reader would have no difficulty linking the two. Lisa Springer said the book's character, "Lisa Blake", was like her physically and, like her, spoke French fluently and loved to ski. But, in something of an arch distinction, the court noted that while Lisa Springer was a tutor, Lisa Blake was independently wealthy.

Allowing Mr Batra's case to proceed to the next stage of litigation, though, Justice Marilyn Shafer said the earlier unsuccessful case was distinguishable from the current one because, unlike Lisa Springer, Mr Barta was a "public figure".

English cases like this are rare, but one of note came in 2000 when Keith Laird sued Channel 4 over an episode of its television programme *Phoenix Nights*. The programme featured a character called "Keith Lard". Like Keith Laird, Keith Lard was a fire officer in Bolton, and had a bushy moustache and a bright yellow jacket. Lard used the same mannerisms as Laird and the same expressions like "It's not fire that kills, it's ignorance". Mr Laird was taunted by Bolton council workers who assumed the television character was based on him. But in something of an embellishment, Lard was shown as having a penchant for sexually interfering with dogs. When Laird's colleagues started calling him "Woof Woof", he called a solicitor. The programme makers eventually agreed to pay £10,000 compensation.

Not dressing down, down under

"She always conducted herself as if short skirts and tight shirts would lead to success", a public commentator said of Zarah Garde-Wilson in 2008.

Known fondly as the Hyphen-with-the-Python after she appeared in a men's magazine posing provocatively with a large snake, Garde-Wilson has drawn some bad reactions from her professional colleagues. That's because Zarah isn't a glamour model. She's a solicitor. Her response? "I believe it's a malicious witch hunt against me purely because of the people I represent".

She is a controversial gangland lawyer in Melbourne, Australia. In 2008 a criminal trial against her collapsed after a key prosecution witness suffered from an acute memory loss.

At the county court, she faced four charges of lying to the Australian Crime Commission (ACC) and possessing an unregistered firearm. The Crown alleged that she lied, when she gave evidence to the ACC in 2004, about the circumstances surrounding the death of her *de facto* husband Lewis Caine.

Caine, a convicted murderer, was shot dead and dumped in a street in a gangland war. Garde-Wilson informed detectives that psychic spirits had told her where Caine was murdered. Prosecutors alleged she lied in telling the ACC she hadn't given Caine's gun to a police informant known as '166', and when she said she hadn't seen a gun at the apartment she shared with Caine. The deception case against Garde-Wilson fell down when '166' told the court he couldn't remember the conversation he had with Ms Garde-Wilson about Caine's gun.

Even though '166' secretly recorded the conversation and admitted he could identify his own voice as it was played to the court, he said, unexpectedly, midway through the trial, that he couldn't recall the event: "I don't remember any of that happening to be honest" he told the court. Puzzled silence all around.

"Was collecting a gun such a common thing that you don't recall collecting a gun from her?", Judge Roland Williams asked him.

"Well, for some people, that's nothing, your Honour", replied '166'.

Outside the court, Ms Garde-Wilson's lawyer Stephen Shirrefs said his client was relieved the case was over. "She just wants her privacy", he said, without disclosing whether she'd be appearing again soon semi-naked in a men's magazine.

Zarah has had many challenging legal encounters. Among these, she was apprehended at a Metropolitan Remand Centre with 100 needles and 125 syringes in her car boot. She claimed the items were for her boyfriend as he used steroids. Clearly, this solicitor's life is not all statutes and scrabble.

She is widely known for her plunging necklines and stilettos. "That's how she dressed on prison visits and appearing in court", one former lawyer has observed, "But in the legal profession, you can dress down and still get there – if you're any good". Certainly, you can, and must in Britain.

Historically, the English Bar has been pretty buttoned-down about the appearance of its members. In the 16th century, the Benchers of Lincoln's Inn banned barristers from having beards. The Bar's current Code of Conduct says that, in court, a barrister's personal appearance should be "decorous", and "his dress, when robes are worn, should be compatible with them".

But it isn't just sexually suggestive dress that British courts forbid. A magistrates' court once refused to hear a male advocate who was wearing brown suede shoes. Knocking him straight into the rough, the Bench condemned the style as better suited to the golf course than a law court.

Legal oaths

A deposition is a sworn statement. It is not a swearing statement. But Aaron Wider, a mortgage company chief executive from Long Island, New York, seems not to have appreciated the difference. In March 2008, he and his lawyer were fined $29,323 for his use of the word "fuck", and its grammatical variants, 73 times during a deposition.

District Court Judge Eduardo Robreno said he had never encountered anything like it in 30 years.

In the filmed deposition, Wider gets off to a robust start when questioned by his opponent's lawyer. Asked some polite questions, Wider instantly rounds on the lawyer snarling "Don't fucking threaten me you arsehole". Later during the deposition the lawyer asks Wider what the letters in his company name, HTFC Corp, stand for. "Hit That Fucking Clown", is the remarkably rapid response (it is really High Tech Financial Corp).

The lawyer at whom Wider directs his wrath on the film is Robert Bodzin. Mr Bodzin represents GMAC Bank of Philadelphia, which was suing HTFC in a contract case. It was alleged that HTFC sold millions of dollars worth of improperly secured home loans. The companies reached a provisional settlement but GMAC then sought to sue Wider personally.

Imposing the fine for the bad language, federal Judge Eduardo Robreno, described Wider's conduct as "outrageous". Wider, however, was quite nonchalant about upgrading his impertinence from lawyer defiance to judicial defiance. Describing his swearing as a "constitutional right", he later audaciously declared that he had no intention of paying the fine the judge had imposed.

He said "I will go down in history as someone who defied the federal government". Then, with rising insolence, he said "I have defied one man who comes from a communist country" (Judge Robreno is America's first Cuban-born federal judge). "If he told Fidel Castro to go fuck himself, he would be in prison".

Mutating from a roaring lion to a timid lamb, though, Wider afterwards called a reporter and asked to retract that statement, saying, "I don't want to go to jail".

The earthy vernacular is sometimes heard in British courts but there are also some cases where the use of language is more sharp than rough. In the Glasgow Sheriff Court in Scotland, when sentencing a local rascal, the judge said "Although you are a fecund liar, I am going to give you one last chance". The accused immediately replied: "That's great your Honour, I always knew you were a fecund good judge".

You may not kiss the bride

The English advocate David Mellor once noted that "lawyers are like rhinoceroses: thick skinned, short-sighted and always ready to charge". The boldness of some lawyers is decidedly unbounded. Consider the attitude of counsel for Gons Gutierrez Nachman.

Nachman, a 42-year-old former US diplomat, was convicted in April 2008 of the serious crime of having had underage sex with three teenage girls while serving as a consular officer in Brazil and Congo. His lawyers, you might think, would have show caution about what to say to the judge before he imposed sentence. As counsel for

Nachman, your best choice might not be, "Would Your Honour agree, please, to conduct a marriage ceremony in this courtroom between my convicted client and his 21-year old Brazilian fiancée?". Yet that is what Mr Nachman's lawyers did indeed ask the judge.

Nachman's lawyers requested that in Alexandria, Virginia, in the same courtroom where he was convicted of the sex crimes, Nachman should be permitted, by District Judge Gerald Bruce Lee, to marry Carolina Pereira Porcher. The lawyers did not, evidently, specify whether the ceremony would involve the bride walking down the aisle of the courtroom hooked to her father's arm to meet Mr Nachman, while he was standing at the head of the court facing the Bench and looking up to the judge. Can you imagine the post-ceremony wedding photos? Would there be one of the judge smiling in the middle of the newly weds, with his arms embracing them both?

Nachman, who made videos of his sex with underage girls, applied to the state for a licence to marry. Once this was granted, his lawyers asked the judge to perform the ceremony. The prosecution objected, saying that the request "attempt[ed] to shift the focus away from the very serious criminal offences for which he will be sentenced". The request was declined, the judge having commented that it would have been absurd to divert attention from a serious case to perform the marriage.

One old definition of *chutzpah* is that it's the sort of audacity shown by a child who, having killed both his parents, asks the judge for clemency because he is an orphan. A modern equivalent might now involve the lawyer who asks the judge to conduct the marriage of the sex convict he's about to sentence.

Litigation school

If this were a movie trailer, a man's deep gravelly voice would say, over a shot of students leaving a law lecture, "When evil is suspected at a law school, the exorcism is litigation".

The Alben W Barkley School of Law (formerly the American Justice School of Law) was founded in 2004, as a private institution in Paducah, Kentucky. It closed on New Year's Eve in 2008. Its demise was foretold when a group of its students filed a $120 million class action lawsuit against the school's administration. In an 82-page document, the suit alleged that the Dean and others had engaged in a breathtaking catalogue of wrongs – including racketeering, conspiracy, theft, wire fraud, mail fraud, extortion and abuse of their offices "to enrich themselves at the expense of the students".

In November 2007, Tom Osborne, a local lawyer who had recently resigned as the school's board chairman, filed the suit on behalf of himself and the students. Apart from $120 million in damages, the suit sought a restraining order to prevent the school from filing for bankruptcy.

The suit claimed the Dean and Associate Dean worked together to delay distribution of student loans so that they could invest the funds and earn interest. The action also asserted that the students would suffer demonstrable loss. Having taken out large loans to pay for their education, their chances of getting a qualifying law degree were remote, given that the school hadn't been accredited by the American Bar Association. The defendants said they'd done nothing wrong and that the claim was encouraged by disgruntled academics who were not given permanent contracts.

It is true that not everything in law schools keeps everyone amused. Sir John Mortimer QC once reflected that when studying at university, "I found the legal syllabus enormously dull and spent as little time at it as possible". But litigation against law schools in England has been very rare and predictably quaint. In a claim against the University of London in 1965, alleging negligence by the law examiners, a student was unable to persuade the Court of Appeal that he deserved better marks. He represented himself – but got the law wrong in arguing his case.

English law schools were once ordered to close down. However, when this happened it wasn't because the schools were bad but because they were seen by the King as dangerously good. Law schools established in London in the early 13th century were shut in 1234 by a writ of Henry III. The writ said:

... Through the whole city of London let it be proclaimed and wholly forbidden that anyone who has a school of law in that town shall teach the laws ... and if anyone shall conduct a school of that nature there, the Mayor and the Sheriffs shall put a stop to it at once.

That was an era when the King had his own special ways of teaching the law to anyone whom he thought in need of some education about how the rules work.

Million dollar question

A law student entering the profession can attract attention for various reasons but publicly proving a prominent lawyer wrong and then suing him for a million dollars is unusual.

During an interview on national television, Cheney Mason, a leading defence lawyer in Florida, was protesting that the multiple-murder case against his convicted client was flawed. He said his client, who had been sentenced to death, could not, as the prosecution alleged, have killed three people in Florida at 5.20pm one day and have appeared on CCTV in a hotel in Atlanta at 10.00pm on that same day. Mason also declared it was impossible for anyone to disembark from an aircraft in Atlanta airport and get to the hotel 5 miles away in less than 28 minutes. He then said "I challenge anybody to show me, I'll pay them a million dollars if they can do it".

Watching that interview was Dustin Kolodziej, a law student from Texas. He later rose to the challenge. Filming himself, he retraced the route used by the murderer. He flew from Atlanta to Orlando (where the killings took place) and back again, and he completed the final airport-to-hotel leg within 28 minutes. He claimed the $1m from Mason on the basis that he'd completed a "unilateral contract". In most contracts the parties agree on terms but in a unilateral contract one party makes an offer, like a reward for the return of lost property, and the other party, a stranger, can complete the contract by simply doing what is asked. Mason refused to pay the

$1m. Kolodziej, who graduated in 2009, sued Mason in the federal court in Texas.

To win, Kolodziej will have to prove that a reasonable person in his position would have assumed Mason's $1m offer was serious. The courts have previously rejected some extravagant unilateral contract claims. In 1996, a Pepsi television advert depicted, along with sun glasses and a leather jacket, a real Harrier fighter jet (cost: $23m) as among the goods claimable with tokens from purchasing drinks. John Leonard sued PepsiCo for the jet when the company wouldn't redeem 7 million 'Pepsi points' he'd acquired for $700,000. The court ruled the fighter jet offer was just in jest. But claimants have sometimes succeeded. In 1967, the Jesse James museum curator asserted that the desperado wasn't killed in 1882 but lived with him in Missouri until the 1950s. On national television he said he'd pay $10,000 to anyone who proved him wrong. A relative of James did so and she won her claim to the money.

A most curious "I'll pay if you prove me wrong" case was decided in England in 1892. The Carbolic Smoke Ball Company promised to pay £100 to anyone who used its product but caught the flu. Elizabeth Carlill, bought the Smoke Ball, used it, got the flu, and won damages. She enjoyed a long life and died 50 years later aged 96, unfortunately, from flu.

Season's pleadings

The principle that "where there's a hit there's a writ" doesn't cease to apply during the season of goodwill.

The novelty song "Grandma Got Run Over by a Reindeer", sung by Elmo Shropshire, became a hit in 1979 and has been popular ever since. But it was a feature not only in the radio play lists but also in the court case lists.

The song generated an animated television show in 2000, and in 2007 Elmo Shropshire was sued for breach of contract by a company that claimed he interfered in a $2 million deal it had made to sell musical trucks, dolls, snow globes and cookie jars featuring characters from the programme.

The song about Santa running down a tipsy grandmother with his sleigh, and the TV spin-off continue to run seasonally worldwide. The Fred Rappoport Co argues it owns the rights to use the song to promote products featuring the characters. It claims it acquired those rights in settlement of a 2004 lawsuit brought by "Dr Elmo" (who was a vet before turning to song). Rappoport claims that Dr Elmo improperly sent cease-and-desist letters to companies with which it had contracted to market products. Dr Elmo says the company can sell any characters from the show, "[b]ut I own the copyright from the song. [Rappoport] can't use the song without my permission". Thus did the temperature rise sharply in the winter wonderland before the case was settled.

The jolliness of Christmas works in almost all venues except courts. Courts cannot do jollity. Just before Christmas, 2000, at Luton Magistrates' Court, a sullen convicted man was about to be sentenced for a property crime when the courtroom suddenly rang out to the tune "Santa Claus is Coming to Town". The magistrate, Hector Graham, awkwardly opened his jacket and began fiddling with his musical novelty Santa Claus tie. The courtroom was aghast. The man in the dock stood dismayed and slack-jawed. The magistrate's tie then burst into "We Wish You a Merry Christmas" before stopping, at which point the defendant was jailed for 4 months.

Sisters in law

An unusual case in Italy, in October 2008, rested on an allegation of double trouble: a woman who posed as her twin sister to argue cases as an advocate in court. Both twins appeared in court together, this time as defendants.

The story began when Gabriela Odisio, an Italian lawyer and part-time judge from Magenta, realised she was double-booked as both an advocate and judge on the same day in different places. She allegedly invited her identical twin, Patrizia, to assume her identity as an advocate and present a case while she went off to act as a judge. This ruse would enable Gabriela, in effect, to draw fees for working in two places at once.

Gabriela and her twin Patrizia – who had a law degree but wasn't an advocate – were accused of sustaining this deception for 3 years in courts in Vigevano and Rho in northern Italy.

When Patrizia appeared in court as Gabriela, wearing her robe, the impersonation was perfect. They are absolutely identical and were said to know everything about each other's lives – and so were allegedly able to fool everyone around them for years. The quality of Patrizia's advocacy was evidently never questioned.

The prosecution said the siblings' scam was only exposed when one of Gabriela's clients overheard her and her sister discussing their plans. The twins were prosecuted for making false statements about qualifications and deceiving clients.

The Italian case arose from Gabriela Odisio being unable to occupy two different legal roles at the same time. There is precedent, though, for an English lawyer being in different legal roles at the same time in the same court.

In August 1989, Eric Bailey was prosecuted at Hendon Magistrates' Court, London, for speeding and driving while disqualified after he was caught racing on a motorway at 102mph. At the hearing, however, the prosecution lawyer failed to arrive. Mr Bailey really didn't want his case postponed so his defence lawyer, Patrick Cusack, asked the court if he could be the advocate for both sides: present the prosecution case and then defend his client. The Bench agreed.

In an imaginative display of legal versatility, Mr Cusack assumed the role of prosecutor against Mr Bailey, giving it his best shot. He then swung into defence mode by giving a plea of mitigation in respect of the offences for which his client pleaded guilty. Mr Bailey was fined £300 and ordered to do 200 hours' community service.

Mr Cusack said he was pleased to have provided the dual services and wouldn't be seeking a "double time" fee. He also said that even though there had been a conviction, he wouldn't, as prosecutor, be asking himself as defence lawyer to cover his prosecution costs.

Mr Cusack's double role stratagem was neat but don't mention it to anyone from the Ministry of Justice – in case they hatch a cost-saving scheme by having just one lawyer in all cases.

Contempt most foul

Lawyers usually benefit from the courts' use of precedent because it's helpful to know that cases will be decided in line with earlier similar cases. But Michael Brautigam, an attorney from Ohio, didn't benefit from the doctrine of precedent. Instead, he was given an immediate jail sentence, in December 2008, when his foul-mouthed contempt of court in a civil case was treated in the same way as that of a gang member in court the previous day.

On being informed by the judge that a trial about gang crime would be set for a date several weeks ahead, a young defendant who was being held in custody expressed his objections in court in a concise and forceful way. He said "That's fucking bullshit". The judge's response was also concise and forceful. He immediately sentenced the young man to 6 months jail for contempt.

The next day, before the same judge, Mr Brautigam was representing himself in a civil action against a property association. He asked the judge for extra time to prepare his case, and he was granted it. A hostility, though, had built up between the lawyers in this case and during one exchange between them Brautigam was heard to call the other attorney a "fucking liar".

The judge cited him for contempt, referred to the 6-month sentence he had given the day before to the gang member for uttering profanities in court. Following precedent, the judge promptly sentenced Brautigam to the same 6 months in custody.

What is sauce for the goose is sauce for the gander, and under Ohio law what is a sentence for the lout is sentence for the lawyer. Cases of lawyers using profanities elsewhere, however, have been treated more leniently. In 2008, Deputy District Judge Esther Cunningham arrived drunk in court in Lincolnshire to act as an advocate for her cousin. She swayed on her feet, forcibly kissed another solicitor in court and used obscene language.

She wasn't jailed but simply barred from practice for 6 months. It might have been an even lighter penalty if she hadn't tried to justify her profanities. When the court usher declined her command to name people in the courtroom, she told him to "fuck off". She then continued to use a variety of four-letter words and sought to invalidate the prosecution by declaring that the Crown Prosecutor was a "fuckwit". That is not a recognised defence in English law. Given an opportunity to comment on her insult, she opted for another inventive argument unlikely to delight the court. She said that it wasn't an unreasonable insult to call the prosecutor a fuckwit – because he had "been called worse things in his time".

D'oh!

Homer has been referred to in English cases many times but such allusions were to the ancient Greek poet. In January 2009, for the first time, a British lawyer cited Homer Simpson in support of an argument he was making in court.

John Walker, a solicitor, was addressing the Bench at Walsall Magistrates' Court. His client, Ricky Hodgkinson, had pleaded guilty to an offence under the Firearms Act 1968 after police had caught him with a Taser gun he'd bought in a pub for £100 for "self-defence". Showing that he had an unconventional understanding of self-defence, the first thing Hodgkinson did with the million-volt stun gun was fire it at his own chest. He said later that he was just testing it to see how powerful it was.

In an effort to mitigate the seriousness of his client's crime, Walker told the court, "He is like the cartoon character Homer Simpson. It was a silly thing for him to do but he hasn't used it on anyone but himself". The lawyer then offered the court more detail, explaining, "There have been scenes in *The Simpsons* when Homer has given himself electric shocks and leapt in the air screaming with his tongue hanging out. This was a bit like that".

Was the comparison a good one for a courtroom lawyer to make? After all, Homer Simpson has himself appeared in courts but has never been treated with great sympathy by judges, despite his lovable ineptitude:

Judge: Your licence is hereby revoked, and I'd like you to attend traffic school and 2 months of Alc-Anon meetings.

Homer: Your honour, I'd like that stricken from the record.

Judge: No.

And Homer's lawyer, Lionel Hutz, is always less than perfect in trying to get Homer off the hook. In one scene he advises a jailed Homer through prison bars:

Hutz: Don't worry, Homer, I've got a foolproof strategy to get you out of here: surprise witnesses, each more surprising than the last. I tell you, the judge won't know what hit him. [but the camera then pulls back to reveal that Hutz himself is imprisoned in the cell next to Homer]

Warder: [bangs bars with nightstick] Pipe down in there, Hutz.

Although Homer is a new entrant to the British courts, he has already appeared in an Australian case. In 1996, the Federal Court heard a commercial case about whether it was legal for a brewery to market a product called Duff Beer. The judge gave a warm description of *The Simpsons*. Homer would have smiled sweetly when the judge ruled that he was "world famous" and "good natured". But the judge's evaluation of him went a bit further, noting that Homer "could not be described as endowed with much intelligence, taste or common sense". D'oh!

Don't Bank on it

Among the things you hear lawyers saying about themselves, "I'm not very good at law" and "I've no assets beyond my clothes and my wedding ring" don't crop up often. Yet that is what Illinois lawyer, James

Gordon Banks, told a court in 2009. He had been found personally liable to pay the costs of his opponent attorney after deliberately expanding a civil action with vexatious allegations.

The lawyer v lawyer dispute arose in a case about a drivers' union election. The losers of the election, represented by Banks, sued the winners alleging that the result was fixed through racketeering. Those allegations soon proved to be unfounded. During the case, the defendants' lawyers had written to Banks, demanding that his unwarranted claims be withdrawn. But Banks did not withdraw the claims and didn't even reply. He continued to bully the defendants.

Once the defendants had won the case, their lawyers applied to have their costs paid by Banks, arguing that they'd had to do lots of unnecessary work because of his vexatious claims. The district court agreed and told Banks to pay the other side's lawyers $80,000, as that sum represented reasonable attorney fees for the amount of unnecessary work they'd had to do. Banks said that he couldn't pay that sum and invited the court to reduce the award against him, pleading that his assets were very limited: $2,000 in cash, a watch, his clothes and his wedding ring.

The seventh circuit Court of Appeals ruled that Banks must pay the $80,000. It reasoned that, as he had committed an intentional tort when he maliciously expanded the litigation, the trial court wasn't bound to examine his personal assets before deciding on the level of compensation to be paid to his victim. It ruled that the sum of damages should depend "on the victim's loss, not the wrongdoer's resources". The court was clear about just how wrong Banks had been in bringing the actions against the winner of the union election: "Instead of hitting [the defendant] with a fist or an insult, [Banks] hit him with a lawsuit".

The court also noted that Banks did seem to enjoy a home, cars and savings, but that these were all in his wife's name. The ruling suggests that if paying the $80,000 would be too much for Banks, he should file for bankruptcy. The bankruptcy court could then examine whether he'd engaged in any fraudulent conveyances of property in order to hide his assets.

Banks tried to excuse himself by saying he was not great at law and had only 4 years' post-qualification experience. But the court wasn't sympathetic. It declared, "If Banks really is a bad lawyer (as he depicts himself), and is poor because people are not willing to pay much, or at all, for his services, then he should turn from the practice of law to some other endeavour where he will do less harm". Other professions might already be warning their gatekeepers about him but, as he is called Banks, the government might have been willing to pump generous rescue money his way without asking too many questions about how it would be used.

Unconventional costs

Having or asking for sex with clients has triggered trouble for lawyers in several cases. In 2004, a barrister from Melbourne had his practising certificate suspended for 6 months after he asked a client for sex during a pre-hearing conference in her home. After giving her a mock cross-examination he indicated he wanted to have sex and when she declined, he looked at her breasts and said "just let me feel those puppies then, they're beautiful". She said she hoped her refusal to have sex wouldn't affect the outcome of her case, and he said it would not but he "would have been happier if we had had sex".

In 2002, a man was standing trial for a macabre triple murder in Washington state when his lawyer, Theresa Olson, a public defender, was witnessed having sexual intercourse with him in an interview room in the King County jail. The defendant was later convicted and she was suspended for 2 years. The television presenter Jay Leno said that "a lawyer in Seattle is in trouble for having sex in jail with her client who is a murderer. How creepy is that, huh? Sex with a lawyer".

Let me through, I'm a lawyer

Lawyers racing to a disaster to procure work is never a morally uplifting sight. In 2005, the Californian Bar, however, developed a scheme which, although it involves

Bar representatives appearing at scenes of devastation, is designed to defeat 'ambulance chasing' lawyers. How it will be seen publicly is another matter.

There was a major train disaster in Glendale, California in 2005. Eleven people died and 180 were injured when an apparently suicidal man drove his car on to the tracks. Straight to the scene, to mingle with emergency service personnel, came a State Bar investigator. Wearing an official windbreaker jacket marked "State Bar of California", he began distributing business cards and pamphlets informing victims about legal representation, and protecting them from individuals who might try to solicit business. The solicitation of clients at the scene of an accident or in a hospital, called "capping", is unlawful in California.

Britain has had chronic problems with 'ambulance chasing' lawyers. A letter to *The Times* in 1912 referred to lawyers' touts who obtained cases by "haunting the side doors of our metropolitan hospitals and buttonholing the distressed relatives of those who have met with accidents". Clients were acquired by "a ghoulish alertness in studying the newspapers for announcements of accidents". The phenomenon was later decried in a 1928 Law Society paper entitled "Ambulance Chasing". It was widespread in the 1950s, and was condemned in a 1964 parliamentary debate. There is today, however, no danger of seeing emergency service lawyers arriving at accidents in siren-blaring limousines.

Hoist by his own canard

If disrespect for a judge reaches the pitch of "scurrilous abuse" it can amount to the crime of contempt of court. In the 1900 case of *R v Gray*, the editor of the *Birmingham Evening Post* was fined £100 with £25 costs for abusing Mr Justice Darling with phraseology which included a reference to the judge as "the impudent little man in horse hair, a microcosm of conceit and empty-headedness".

Meanwhile, some of our Australian brethren are made of sterner stuff. The Supreme Court of Victoria held in 1999 that it was not contempt of court for a solicitor, when served with an injunction, to say: "Justice Beach has got his hand on his dick". The court held that:

... The matter must be judged by contemporary Australian standards. It may be offensive, but it is not contempt of court, for a person to describe a judge as a wanker. The words uttered by the defendant, albeit particularised, say just that. The words spoken by the defendant do not undermine confidence in the administration of justice. They undermine confidence in the persona of the solicitor who spoke them ...

The Supreme Court, in effect, flicked away the intended insult and told the lawyer his abuse had rebounded back on him.

The uncommon scents of justice

The Bar in Iasi, Romania, demanded £1 million compensation from the state in 2005 for the allegedly humiliating conditions in which lawyers in the courts have to work. Marianna Bazdara, representing 600 lawyers, argued that advocates had had enough of the "pestilential smell" in court rooms that "look like either cellars or stables and have no fresh air flowing in them". Historically, in Britain, the earliest arbitrations were open air events. Early indoors hearings were not always salubrious. King Alfred once dealt with a lawsuit in Wiltshire as he was "in his chamber, washing his hands". Later, English law courts were commonly neither luxurious nor even plumbed. In 1848, Chief Baron Pollock recounted that "in our older Courts of Justice, the judge retired to the corner of the room for a necessary purpose, even in the presence of ladies". The aromatic atmosphere for court business would thus often vaporise from a judicial porcelain vase.

Lost in litigation

How bad does a lawyer's courtroom performance have to be before a judge will order a retrial? This question was answered by a court in New York in 2009 when Edward

Trujillo appealed against a firearms conviction, saying that his defence lawyer had spent the trial sleeping, reading a magazine and making irrelevant speeches.

In New York, citizens are legally entitled to a standard of advocacy set at "meaningful representation". The law is not only to protect individual defendants; it is also to ensure that the justice system itself isn't brought into disrepute by unprofessional conduct.

After being convicted, Trujillo submitted an affidavit swearing that during the trial his counsel fell asleep three times, spent significant periods of the trial, when he wasn't asleep, reading health and fitness magazines, and made several eccentric speeches which did not seem to be related to the case at all. Those included an opening speech which caused the jury to laugh at the defence. In hearing an appeal for a retrial, the original trial judge said he had noticed counsel asleep, had witnessed him drop a magazine on the floor during the case, and heard the lawyer's "bizarre opening statement" which triggered an outburst of hilarity in court. The judge said he found himself "uncomfortable" whenever Trujillo's lawyer addressed a witness or the jury as, "It was impossible to predict what he was going to say".

Trujillo won his appeal for a retrial. The court held that the quality of representation he got was so insufficient that "the integrity of the judicial process was placed in jeopardy". That inappropriate courtroom conduct is, though, trumped by the less than effective representation of attorney Raymond Brownlow who was charged with contempt of court in the District of Columbia in 1968. He had arrived in court in the late morning and had begun to address the judge in a most erratic way in front of a bemused client. This exchange then followed:

Judge: Have you been drinking?
Brownlow: I had a cocktail at lunch
Judge: This morning?
Brownlow: Yes,

The first thing to draw the suspicion of the judge, however, was the fact that Brownlow was appearing in the wrong case – the opening speech into which he'd loudly launched was for a different trial being held in another courtroom.

Chapter 9

Jurors, Friends and Neighbours

A courtroom is an assembly of tense people in great formality gathered to play a drama with an end that isn't yet written but which is very important for several people there. But the tight formality is often broken by the simplest of human errors:

Judge:	Is there any reason why you cannot be empanelled as a juror on this case?
Prospective juror:	I must not be away from my job for a long time
Judge:	Can't they do without you at your work?
Prospective juror:	Yes, but I don't want them to know that.

People can end up in the most extraordinary situations as they become involved in court cases.

I think he's not guilty

There is an old adage: "Be kind to everybody – you never know who might show up on the jury at your trial".

Ideally, of course, if you were being tried, you'd want the jury to be as reasonable as you are. And that's just how things worked out for Pierre Piasco. In July 2008, he was going to be tried for murder in France – despite having been summoned to serve on the jury in his own trial.

Mr Piasco had been accused of a murder in Aix-en-Provence. He was alleged to have shot Christian Vaidié with a 357 Smith and Wesson, a weapon he was later caught carrying. Asked about whether he'd accept the jury summons, he had said he would honour his civic duty by accepting the state's invitation.

But being the lone juror who promotes nagging doubt in the minds of a conviction-hungry jury, like Peter Fonda in *12 Angry Men*, wouldn't work well if the man saying "but what if this is all just a big mistake" is sitting in the dock.

The trial was set down for September 2008 at the Assize Court of Bouches-du-Rhone, when both sides had a chance to review the jury composition. After legal arguments, Mr Piacso was eventually asked to stand down as a prospective juror although this was not because he might be biased but rather because he was, under Article 256 the French Penal Code, a "detained person" and therefore unable to serve.

Judging yourself has been allowed in some cases in England – but only if you're a judge. In 1846, Mr Justice Maule was an appeal judge in a civil case that he had presided over in Northampton as the trial judge. Looking back at his own trial judgment, he said "I think I was wrong". But the other appeal judges disagreed with him. They said his original judgment had been right, so it stood as it was.

This practice of sitting on appeal on your own judgment has also been allowed in the United States. In 1847, Justice Bronson said that a judge was "wise enough to know he is fallible". He went on to suggest, somewhat bizarrely, that a judge "is the very best man to sit in review upon his own judgments". You get the feeling that litigants who left his courtroom aggrieved with his judging wouldn't have been delighted with the Bronson formula for the best way to run an appeal process.

People have sometimes appeared in the same case in two capacities. In 1985, Oresti Lodi sued himself in California in an unsuccessful attempt to gain a tax advantage but his action was dismissed by Shasta County Superior Court as a "slam-dunk frivolous complaint".

Self-trial has also been recorded. Francis Evans Cornish was appointed Queen's Counsel in Canada in 1857, when aged 26. He became Winnipeg's first elected Mayor in 1874 which gave him status as a magistrate. Arrested one evening by the police for being drunk in public, Cornish was ordered to appear later before a magistrate, and that magistrate turned out to be ... himself. Sober by now, he convicted himself and fined himself $5 with costs. But he was a fair and even-handed magistrate, always keen to see both sides of a case. He stated for the record: "Francis Evans Cornish, taking into consideration past good behaviour, your fine is remitted".

Eleven angry men

Serving on a jury is an important civic duty. In America, however, about half of all people summoned do not serve or get excused duty. Most people seeking an excusal fill out the application form politely, but Erik Slye from Gallatin County, Montana, took a different approach.

In response to the call to duty in 2009, Slye's initial abrupt reply saying he would not serve was rejected by the court. He was contacted in writing again, with an explanation that he must serve unless he could show that doing so would cause him "undue hardship". Slye then submitted a sworn affidavit to the court officials and judge and began with a certain robust clarity: "Apparently you morons didn't understand me the first time".

He explained that he could not take time off work, and gave his reason as being "I am not putting my family's well-being at stake to participate in this crap". He asserted "I do not believe in our 'justice' system". Then, going into what he must have thought was helpful detail for the court, Mr Slye next stated in his affidavit that "Jury service is a complete waste of time". He added, in case there was any lingering doubt among the jury summoning officers, "I would rather count the wrinkles on my dog's balls than sit on a jury. Get it through your thick skulls. Leave me the Fuck alone".

This was something of a tactical error on Mr Slye's part because no affidavit could have been better composed than the one he sent to achieve just what he didn't want. He was not left alone by the court but, under threat of jail, summoned by the judge to appear and ordered to make a humbling personal apology to all the court officials.

Over time there have been many remarkable excuses offered to courts by prospective jurors who wanted to escape jury duty. These have included one from New Jersey in which the applicant stated, "I am a professional psychic so I would know who is guilty even before the trial" – the excuse was rejected, but I guess she saw that coming. Another letter from New Jersey was posted by an applicant who said he needed to "attend a St Patrick's Day party" – also rejected.

In Manhattan, a paralegal who had missed jury service was summoned to court to explain. She said her work for her law firm had been too important to ignore. As proof, she brought a lawyer from her firm to explain the hectic situation to the judge. Her court business was found to be more important than the law firm business, so she was immediately fined $250 and ordered to serve on the next jury.

The prize in the category of 'international best excuse for being allowed to miss jury duty' must go to a Mr ACL Blair from London who was called to serve as a juror in 2000. He had several reasons for not spending 2 weeks listening to cases – but his main one was that he was too busy being the British Prime Minister.

The sleeping juror

The attention of some jurors is curiously difficult to maintain. An obscenity trial in Cincinnati in 2003 was halted during a courtroom showing of the pornographic film *Maximum Hardcore Extreme, Vol. 7*, when a member of the jury fell asleep. Judge Richard Niehaus declared a mistrial, observing that "justice requires the evidence to be reviewed and considered in its entirety".

Under English law, if a juror falls asleep, it is for the judge to decide at the time whether to discharge the sleeper or the whole jury or simply to proceed. In a case in 1997, a juror had fallen asleep during the judge's summing up in a trial for the importation of cocaine. The judge then asked the freshly awoken juror how much he had missed, to which the reply was "very little" so the judge proceeded without further action. The convicted defendant's appeal that the conviction was "unsafe" failed because no objection had been made at the time of the incident. In a case in 1976, it emerged that the ears of one of the jurors was "too full of wax to hear half of the evidence, or any of the summing up". However, section 18 of the Juries Act 1974 prevents the reversal of a verdict on the ground "that any juror was unfit to serve" so the unanimous verdict of "guilty" in that case could not be invalidated.

A trial too far

Some trials are dramatic and sensational but jurors cannot always rely on getting a stimulating case to hear. In May 2009, Grant Faber, a juror in Oregon, left the case he was hearing at lunch time and did not go back in the afternoon because, as he told police when they later apprehended him, he was "extremely bored" in court.

Tedium, though, is not a recognised excuse for abandoning jury duty. In an interview with the police who had been despatched with an arrest warrant from the judge, Faber said he found the proceedings at Washington County Courthouse so dull that he "just couldn't take it anymore". His interest in legal proceedings, however, seemed to perk up considerably when the officers explained to him the charge of contempt of court that he would be facing.

Bored jurors have been in trouble before in many jurisdictions. In Sydney, in 2008, a major drug conspiracy case had been running for 66 days and had cost the taxpayer about one million Australian dollars. The judge aborted the trial because it had become evident that five jurors had been playing Sudoku during the proceedings. It was only after 105 witnesses had given evidence, that someone noticed the jurors were apparently taking notes vertically rather than horizontally, and then their pastime was exposed.

It is not only jurors who get bored. Sir Lewis Cave (an English High Court judge 1881–97) was prone to doze off on the Bench during what for him were the less interesting parts of his cases. The techniques used by barristers to awaken him during their speeches included dropping heavy law books on the floor and banging the flaps of their seats.

Through centuries of legal education, there have been occasional instances of students finding law lectures dull. In the gentlemen's toilet of one Law School there is written neatly on the wall, "For the latest lecture of Dr Blank, please press the button", with an arrow pointing to the hand-drying machine.

In issuing a warrant for Grant Faber, the Oregon juror who didn't come back in the afternoon, the judge did the right thing. There are, however, worse cases of courtroom absenteeism. In 1981, Alexander Steel was on trial for robbery in London. He requested bail to leave the court at lunchtime. Benevolently, the judge agreed but warned the defendant of the absolute need to return in the afternoon. "If you do not turn up" the judge declared, "you will make me look a proper Charlie". That night, police were still searching for Mr Steel.

Troublesome ticket testimony

In Ontario, the Superior Court of Justice decided a case in 2009 in which two street drug dealers fought over a $5 million winning lottery ticket. Justice Joseph W Quinn said "during this trial truth was only an occasional visitor" and he noted that "if this ticket were a child and the parties vying for custody, I would find them both unfit and bring in Family and Children's Services". But this was a property case and someone had to win.

In 2006, "after a busy day conducting illegal drugs transactions", Daniel 'Ears' Carley was driven to a shop in St Catharines from which he purchased 12 lottery tickets. He got back into the car where Paul Miller, the driver and his friend since childhood, scratched one of the tickets to discover it was a winning ticket. Ears banked the $5 million and Miller sued, arguing that he had given $10 to Ears just before the key purchase and said "Here, buy me one too".

The judge censured the claimant and defendant. Denying that Miller had been manipulated out of the money by a superior intellect, the judge said, "I do not agree that Ears was the brains of this duo". The judge castigated Miller as a "horrible witness", and noted that although Ears had "many credibility issues", he ultimately seemed to have the more believable account (that he'd bought all the tickets with his own money). Judicial sympathy was reserved for only one witness: Ears' mother. On the night of the win, "true to her British heritage" (she was born in England) she left the celebrations at 7.00pm to watch the soap opera *Coronation Street*. "There was a limit" the judge dryly noted, "to the disruption that she would allow $5 million to make in her life".

The judge ruled that Miller's story of having given $10 for a ticket was a "brazen fabrication" and that Ears was entitled to keep all the winnings. Well, what was left of that sum that is, as he'd been spending it at the rate of $20,000 a week for 3 years.

That, though, wasn't the first time a court has been challenged by a lottery. In Spain, Juan Antonio Roca was arrested for taking systematic bribes as head of urban planning in Marbella. His net salary was less than €150,000 a year, yet when he was arrested his property included two huge Andalusian estates, luxury hotels, three palaces, beachside housing developments, a private plane, and artworks, and was worth in total €2.4 billion. Asked by a judge to explain this wealth, Roca said he had won the lottery 80 times. The prosecution noted that the chances of that were one in 43 quadrillion. In such circumstances, even the best defence lawyer might falter a little when beginning a speech along the lines of: "Improbable as it might seem …".

Evidence weighted against him

"The noise was so loud I thought he had an angle grinder up there", Doris Fox, 68, told Thanet Magistrates' Court, Kent, in April 2008.

In the dock stood Giran Jobe, 36, weighing in at 15 stone.

Although grunting is not a specific offence under English law, Mr Jobe's regular grunts had become unbearable to his neighbours – that and the noise emitted when his bodybuilder power weights came crashing down on the carpet of his top-floor apartment in Margate.

The carpenter was unusually keen on exercising with weights and his regular 2-hour sessions at night could register noise as high a 100 decibels (the level of noise at a platform of an underground station when a train arrives).

After an initial complaint from neighbours to the local authority, Mr Jobe was issued with a noise abatement order. But soon after that new complaints were filed at Thanet Council. Investigators were sent to the downstairs homes to install recorders which monitored Mr Jobe's activity registered the decibel levels.

During the following 6 months, families living below Mr Jobe recorded 47 breaches of the noise abatement order. The offending sounds were cited as "grunting" and "noise from the weights hitting the floor". Mr Jobe was fined £70. He pledged to focus on push-ups.

Other proceedings about more usual noise haven't been successful. In a civil action in 1999, the House of Lords decided that the ordinary use of residential premises wasn't itself capable of being a nuisance. It followed that local authority landlords – in that case, Southwark and Camden Councils – hadn't breached their covenants to tenants for what is quaintly known in law as "quiet enjoyment" of the leased properties.

One of the tenants in the blocks that was not sound-proofed had testified that she could hear "all the private and most intimate moments" of her neighbours' lives. This included "what TV station they are viewing, when they go to the toilet, when they make love". But the court said that these things should have been contemplated by the tenants when they moved into the flats. Another tenant testified that she could hear "singing, arguments, the television, snoring, coughing, bringing up of phlegm, sneezing, bedsprings, footfalls and creaking floorboards, the pull-cord light switch in the bathroom, taps running in the bathroom and kitchen, the toilet being used … the vacuum cleaner and ... music played on the stereo". A judicially endorsed soundtrack of domestic Britain.

Love, law and Lesbos

In June 2008, a civil claim was filed in Athens, Greece, which identified the harm at issue as "psychological and moral rape".

That is an unusual type of injury which might leave many lawyers wondering whom best to ask about what it means: a general practice doctor, a psychiatrist – or even a philosopher.

But the claim got even trickier as it transpired that the alleged victim was not one person but the residents of the island of Lesbos.

Dimitris Lambrou, along with another Lesbos resident and a member of a nationalist pagan association, commenced a legal action to gain the exclusive right to call themselves Lesbians. Their legal action sought to prohibit the Greek Gay and Lesbian Union (OLKE) from using the name 'lesbian'. The group filed the case against the Greek Homosexual and Lesbian Association. The claimants argued that what they saw as the "seizure" of the term 'lesbian' to mean more than simply 'of the island of Lesbos' (in the northern part of the Grecian archipelago) had caused them mental distress.

That legal action, which was eventually rejected by the courts, asked the law to run against a long established usage. Historically, the island of Lesbos became associated with the love poems of the poetess Sappho (born in the 7th century BC), who expressed her love of other women in verses. She was first described as a sexual lover of women in post-classical times.

The word 'lesbianism' appeared in formal English as a term describing sexual orientation in 1870. Lesbianism between consenting people over 16 isn't illegal in English law, and never has been. It is sometimes said that Queen Victoria refused to assent to section 11 of the Criminal Law Amendment Act 1885, which criminalised homosexual conduct, unless all references to women were removed. She didn't believe females did such things. But that story is apocryphal. In 1921, fretful MPs decided not to legislate against lesbianism in case *publication* of such a law introduced "perfectly innocent people" to such relationships.

Renaming Satan

The name someone is given at birth is one of the least important things about them. As Juliet says "What's in a name? That which we call a rose/By any other name would smell as sweet".

But exceptions make the rule. In a child custody hearing in New Plymouth, New Zealand, it materialised that the name of the 9-year-old girl in the case was "Talula Does The Hula From Hawaii".

She told people to call her "K" as she was so ashamed of her real name. Very sensibly, Judge Murfitt decided that the name the parents had given their daughter was "a form of abuse". He put her under the guardianship of the court in order that her name could be changed.

In New Zealand, section 18 of the Births, Deaths and Marriages Registration Act 1995 allows the Registrar to refuse registration if it might "cause offence to a reasonable person" or if it is unreasonably long. A name can also be refused if it resembles an official title or rank, so first names like "The Right Honourable Liam" or "Justice Judith" cannot be registered.

Judge Murfitt ruled that the court was "profoundly concerned about the very poor judgment which this child's parents have shown in choosing this name". He said, "It makes a fool of the child and sets her up with a social disability and handicap, unnecessarily".

He noted that this case was part of a wider phenomenon, and that family courts were becoming dismayed by the eccentricity of names that parents in recent times had given children. These included "Number 16 Bus Shelter" and, for twins, "Benson and Hedges" and "Fish and Chips". Other names that had come to the attention of the courts were: Satan, Hitler, Sex Fruit, and 4Real. The judge noted that the first task of parenthood was not a time "to be frivolous or to create a hurdle for their child's future life".

Other jurisdictions have experienced similar challenges. In 2004, Sara Leisten, of Gothenburg, Sweden, was refused permission to call her son Superman (Staalman). She had chosen the name as he was born with one arm raised above his head, the position in which superman flies. Oddly, however, the Swedish registration office had permitted the names Tarzan and Batman.

In Zhengzhou, Henan province, China a father was refused permission to name his son "@" after the keyboard character. Permission was declined on the legal basis that all names must be capable of being translated into Mandarin.

The English authorities are more lax, especially where a person wants to rename himself. In 1995, Michael Howerd, a marketing consultant from Leeds, was charged £20 by his bank for a £10 overdraft excess. He got into a furious row with the bank and then went to a solicitor and changed his name by deed poll to 'Yorkshire Bank plc Are Fascist Bastards'. He said "I have 69p left in my account and I want the bank to return it by cheque in my full new name".

You haven't gotta have Faith

Wonderwall by Oasis and *Faith* by George Michael, are by common consensus excellent songs. When they are played, however, by buskers James Ryan (on guitar) and Andrew Cave (on dustbin lids) they lose their appeal. And when they are played by that duo incessantly every day until the early hours of the morning, local residents lose the will to live.

In a case at Birmingham Magistrates' Court in 2009, Ryan and Cave were prosecuted for playing those songs, and only those songs, until local people could not bear it any longer. Both songs were played loudly, wailingly, out of tune, and in a continuous sequence. One local resident had to make over 60 formal complaints to police. Another traumatised local man testified that hearing the real songs now triggered severe reactions, "I break down every time I hear *Wonderwall* or the intro to *Faith*".

The court imposed anti-social behaviour orders on both men, excluding them from large areas of the city and banning them from playing musical instruments in public for 2 years. It is hoped that the Supreme Court will not be asked, on an appeal, to judge whether dustbin lids are a musical instrument. The court orders will, though, if nothing else, enable Ryan and Cave to spend time practising and extending their repertoire.

It isn't, however, only ordinary citizens who have provoked legal trouble with their street music. In 2002, Valerie Faure, a French lawyer, faced a professional disciplinary tribunal after being caught busking with an accordion on the streets of Bergerac with her case laid open on the pavement for tips. The allegation was not that her accordion playing was discordant but that she had failed to uphold the legal profession's "principles of honour and morality" by playing music in the street and "soliciting the generosity of the public". Her lawyer claimed the charge against her was unfair. He noted that another French lawyer, Arno Klarsfeld, had not been proceeded against after he'd posed naked on a motorcycle in *Paris Match*. Nonetheless, the tribunal found Faure guilty of bringing the profession into disrepute by busking and suspended her for 6 months.

In 2003, the appeal court in south western Bordeaux overturned that decision on the ground that at the time of the accordion performances Ms Faure wasn't wearing her lawyer's robes and therefore could not have undermined the dignity of the profession. It follows from that reasoning – in which everything hinges on whether a person is visibly a lawyer – that any lawyers wishing to pose for erotic photographs on motorcycles and avoid being disbarred must pose completely naked with no 'fig leaf' cover-ups made from giveaway legal apparel such as robes, wigs, bands or sashes.

Inter Milan 0 – Napoli 2

In Italy, if you are a Napoli football fan, you cannot expect to win away when playing the champions Inter Milan. But that's just on the pitch. In a law court, victory can more easily be achieved.

In 2008, a court in Naples ordered Inter to pay a Napoli fan €1,500 (£1,190) compensation for "existential damage" caused by banners displayed during a match which described Naples as the "sewer of Italy". The insult, part of a general vilification inflicted on Napoli fans at the San Siro stadium in 2007, referred to a chronic refuse crisis that had left rubbish rotting in the streets of Naples.

Provocative abuse was displayed on other banners at the match, which Inter won 2–1, including ones reading "Ciao cholera sufferers!" and "Neapolitans have tuberculosis". Inter fans also sang offensive chants. Raffaele Di Monda, representing the Napoli fan (identified only as GDB), had argued that the concerted and vindictive abuse had made his client feel "indignant and deeply hurt".

Inter had previously been punished by the Italian league for the conduct of its supporters at the match. Sections of the club's stadium in which the banners had been displayed were closed for their following home game. The victory of Mr GDB was the first case in which damages had been claimed for the events at the San Siro. Apart from the damages, the court in Naples also ordered Inter to pay the fan's legal costs, so the courtroom contest went 2–0 to Naples.

Court cases in which it's proved that a whole class of people, like Neapolitans, has been slandered aren't common. One group, though, you'd want to think twice before insulting is lawyers. In a case in Scotland in 1781, a paper had published an article referring indirectly to the Worshipful Society of Solicitors as the "Worshipful Society of Chaldeans [magicians and occultists], Cadies [errand boys] or Running-Stationers ...". You can see where this is going. The Worshipful Society of Solicitors drafted a writ faster than you can say abracadabra.

James Boswell represented the paper's editor, and Dr Johnson wrote the defence for him. Boswell argued that no compensation should be paid to the solicitors because since the mischievous advert had been published they'd not lost any money in fees and so they'd suffered no financial harm. Turning to the alleged injured reputation of solicitors he asked, rather mercilessly, "What is their reputation but an instrument of getting money?". Of the various locations in which insults to the legal profession can be delivered, even by a barrister, a law court isn't a good choice. The court awarded damages to the insulted solicitors and the newspaper editor had to pick up all their decidedly worshipful legal costs.

It's perfectly normal

For failing to return a library book, JoAn Karkos from Maine was taken to court in 2008. She had borrowed a sex education book from the public library in Lewiston but having decided the contents were "dangerous" for children, and having failed to get the police to make obscenity charges, she opted to take censorship into her own hands by declaring her intention to keep the book.

The book is called *It's Perfectly Normal: Changing Bodies, Growing Up, Sex and Sexual Health*. It features candid cartoon illustrations on topics such as abstinence, masturbation, and sexually-transmitted diseases. Written by Robie H Harris and illustrated by Michael Emberley, it has won various educational awards and has been translated into 21 languages since 1993. Ms Karkos, however, took the view that despite the fact that in Lewiston the book had been the subject of only one reader complaint in 13 years, the 36,000 citizens of the town should be prevented from reading it.

Before Judge Valerie Stanfill in the 8th District Court, Ms Karkos admitted that she had the book with her but she refused to hand it over. She was ordered to pay a $100 fine, and eventually allowed to leave court. The authorities decided there was no point in jailing her and allowing her to become a celebrated sufferer for a cause.

Historically, there has been a serious problem for those who try to use the law to ban books: their action is commonly counter-productive. Nothing so effectively enlarges a book's readership as a censor trying to stop people from reading it. It's perfectly normal. As soon as the public in America became aware of the Ms Karkos case, and that she had retained the book, people from all round the country sent their copies to the public library in Lewiston.

In 1960, the publishers of DH Lawrence's *Lady Chatterley's Lover* were prosecuted for obscenity. The prosecutor argued that the book wasn't fit for ordinary people to read, saying it "commends sensuality almost as a virtue". He denied the book had literary merit, dismissed the favourable opinions of distinguished writers and critics, and said the book's characters were just "bodies which continuously had sexual intercourse with one another". The jury acquitted the publishers and the novel sold 3 million copies in a year.

Even bad books can get propelled into popularity by legal attempts to suppress them. In 1986, Peter Wright, a former British secret agent, broke a hallowed code of conduct by publishing his memoirs in a book called *Spycatcher*. He did this having been denied the pension he had expected. Even though the book dwelt on quite stale matters like outdated spy technologies and dead people, and even though the book had already been published in America, the British government resorted to the law to ban the book. There followed 2 years of global litigation and feverish interest in the volume. The result was that a book later described by one law lord as "a literary work of almost unparalleled tedium and banality" became a best seller in many countries and sold over a million copies.

Index